PRAISE FOR
it's prayer time!

If our nation is to be turned to God and to good, the Church must be revived and renewed in commitment and power. If the Church is to approach its potential, it must pray. This book may be a significant factor in bringing revival and renewal to the Church and life to our nation.

Bishop Charles Blake

SENIOR PASTOR, WEST ANGELES CHURCH OF GOD IN CHRIST
LOS ANGELES, CALIFORNIA

Authentic reconciliation and spiritual renewal are major needs of the Church. This book speaks powerfully about those subjects, not only to the reader's mind, but also to our hearts and our feet. Read it and respond humbly and prayerfully to its potent message.

Paul A. Cedar

CHAIRMAN, MISSION AMERICA
PALM DESERT, CALIFORNIA

I can't say enough to describe my gratitude for Mark Pollard's vision and passion. The awakening of spiritual leaders and their flocks to partnership across all lines of historic division is being answered. Here we are served with a classical piece of practical yet scholarly study that summons us to decision. We're not only to pray—we're to pray together!!

Jack W. Hayford

PRESIDENT, THE KING'S SEMINARY
FOUNDING PASTOR, THE CHURCH ON THE WAY
VAN NUYS, CALIFORNIA

Everyone, regardless of race, needs to read this eye-opening and revelatory book. God will use it as a bridge to bring together many communities of people.

Cindy Jacobs
COFOUNDER, GENERALS OF INTERCESSION
COLORADO SPRINGS, COLORADO

What a wonderfully powerful weapon for such a time as this. Amen to *It's Prayer Time!*

Rev. Alveda Celeste King
FOUNDER, KING FOR AMERICA
ATLANTA, GEORGIA

Mark Pollard is a man of true integrity and deep passion for Christ and His kingdom. I strongly support his call to the Body of Christ to fervency and unity in prayer, and trust it will echo loudly throughout our land.

Bill McCartney
FOUNDER AND PRESIDENT, PROMISE KEEPERS
DENVER, COLORADO

It's Prayer Time! is a God-sent book that calls us away from the consumer Christianity of religious entertainment to the conquering Christianity which leads to radical empowerment. This important book will equip you to kick in the gates of hell and reclaim and recover all the enemy has taken in your city. It's prayer time—let's get it on!

Frank M. Reid III
SENIOR PASTOR, BETHEL A.M.E. CHURCH
BALTIMORE, MARYLAND

it's prayer time!

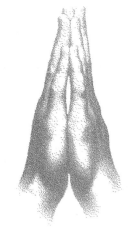

PRAYER & SPIRITUAL WARFARE FROM
THE AFRICAN-AMERICAN PERSPECTIVE

MARK POLLARD,
GENERAL EDITOR

Regal
FROM GOSPEL LIGHT

Published by Regal Books
A Division of Gospel Light
Ventura, California, U.S.A.
Printed in U.S.A.

Regal Books is a ministry of Gospel Light, an evangelical Christian publisher dedicated to serving the local church. We believe God's vision for Gospel Light is to provide church leaders with biblical, user-friendly materials that will help them evangelize, disciple and minister to children, youth and families.

It is our prayer that this Regal book will help you discover biblical truth for your own life and help you meet the needs of others. May God richly bless you.

For a free catalog of resources from Regal Books/Gospel Light, please call your Christian supplier or contact us at 1-800-4-GOSPEL or www.regalbooks.com.

All Scripture quotations, unless otherwise indicated, are taken from the *New King James Version*. Copyright © 1979, 1980, 1982 by Thomas Nelson, Inc. Used by permission. All rights reserved.

Other versions used are:
AMP—Scripture taken from THE AMPLIFIED BIBLE, Old Testament copyright © 1965, 1987 by the Zondervan Corporation. The Amplified New Testament copyright © 1958, 1987 by The Lockman Foundation. Used by permission.
KJV—*King James Version*. Authorized King James Version.
NIV—Scripture taken from the *Holy Bible, New International Version*®. Copyright © 1973, 1978, 1984 by International Bible Society. Used by permission of Zondervan Publishing House. All rights reserved.
RSV—From the *Revised Standard Version* of the Bible, copyright 1946, 1952, and 1971 by the Division of Christian Education of the National Council of the Churches of Christ in the U.S.A. Used by permission.

Cover Design by Kevin Keller
Interior Design by Rob Williams
Edited by Ron Durham and Deena Davis

LIBRARY OF CONGRESS CATALOGING-IN-PUBLICATION DATA
It's prayer time! / Mark Pollard, general editor.
     p. cm.
   Includes bibliographical references.
   ISBN 0-8307-2532-6
   1. Prayer—Christianity. 2. Spiritual warfare. 3. Afro-Americans—Religion. I. Pollard,
     Mark, 1958-

BV210.2.I88 2000
248.3'2—dc21   00-028605

1 2 3 4 5 6 7 8 9 10 11 12 13 14 15 / 09 08 07 06 05 04 03 02 01 00

Rights for publishing this book in other languages are contracted by Gospel Literature International (GLINT). GLINT also provides technical help for the adaptation, translation and publishing of Bible study resources and books in scores of languages worldwide. For further information, contact GLINT, P.O. Box 4060, Ontario, CA 91761-1003, U.S.A. You may also send e-mail to Glintint@aol.com, or visit their website at www.glint.org.

This book is dedicated to Dr. Elliott Mason,
my spiritual mentor;

and to the memories of Rev. Sanford Smith,
a CME pastor and prayer warrior;

and Mother Dabney,
our prayer and spiritual warfare "Elijah."

CONTENTS

A Family Perspective:

*A Father's Commitment to Overcome
Personal Strongholds*
Edgar D. Barron

A Congregational Perspective:

Building a Praying Church
Jerome McNeil, Jr.

A Pastoral Perspective:

Perfecting Passionate Proclamation Through Prayer
Carison Adams

A Personal Perspective:

The Prayer That Heals Abuse
Donn Charles Thomas

Living Beyond Your Hurts
Georgia Ellis

A Leadership Perspective:

Preface

He shall see the fruit of the travail of his soul and be satisfied.
Isaiah 53:11, *RSV*

"Travail" means laborious, strenuous work. Many times this word is used in association with the time preceding birth. Jesus travailed for the soul of humanity. He agonized in prayer during his time in the Garden of Gethsemane. He didn't give up.

This book, written by a diverse network of prayer and spiritual warriors, is a result of generations of travail. Our role has been to midwife the delivery of a dormant vision and impending dream. The vision was foreshadowed by the citywide and national prayer impact of Mother Dabney, a spiritual giant from the Philadelphia area, affiliated with the Church of God in Christ. Years ago, before her untimely death, she held corporate prayer meetings where people came from across the city and nation to encounter the power and presence of God. The dream was gestated in the spirit of Dr. Elliot Mason, whose widespread ministry of prayer and mentoring has deepened the devotional lives of and brought renewal to countless leaders. The dream and vision were of a powerful corporate prayer movement leading to renewal and revival among urban leaders.

This effort seeks to build upon this foundation by providing a voice and vehicle for leaders committed to prayer to collectively affirm that dreams do come true. We continue to travail in prayer for those who would benefit from this united labor of love in print and prophecy. *Our prayer is that you will be drawn into the movement.*

Contrary to the popular perception, not all black churches worship with utter abandon, with the pastor and parishioners continually jumping and shouting in rapturous praise.

My home church, Central Metropolitan CME Church in Jacksonville, Florida, was warm but fairly subdued. Periodically, Sister Williams would fall under the influence of the Spirit, and she would pace back and forth behind the pews. And there was Brother Walden, whose booming "Amen!" and "True enough this morning!" exclamations could overshadow and disrupt the pastor's preaching cadence and often provided comic relief to the kids in the congregation. Central CME is much more expressive and celebrative now, but when I was a teenager, we were indeed "Methodist"—generally mellow and methodical. Prayer at Central was led by a minister or layman who prayed during the invocation.

This was one of the moments when the church shed its mellowness. As I later learned during my early ministerial training, you didn't come to this time playing around; you'd better pray like you needed something from God, and you needed it yesterday. Your passion was acknowledged by a hearty "Amen!" "Pray, son!" or "Yes, sir!" from the church. These times impacted me deeply and increased my appreciation for the power of leading congregational prayer and the sacredness of worship.

In high school, I met several 'saved' young ladies in high school who attended the local Pentecostal church—Holy Temple Church of God in Christ. I would sneak over to Holy Temple's Sunday night service from time to time. I remember the pastor, Bishop C. D. Kinsey, proclaiming in a raspy wail, "It's prayer time!" and the members would rush to the altar en masse. As Bishop Kinsey prayed, the shouts of "Yea, Lord!" "Thank ya, Jesus!" and "Glory to God!" seemed to gradually crescendo and build up to such an intensity that at any moment I expected the roof to simply blow off. And it seemed like the words of the pastor would literally hit the worshipers as he prayed and exclaimed, "God, right now . . . move by your Spirit." These altar calls and services also impacted me as I gained a love for corporate prayer and expressive praise.

As you encounter the words of the ministers and laymen in this book, who represent the rich diversity of the African-American church experience, *our prayer is that you will be impacted.*

The story of a fisherman's family was told by a leading pastor and church leader. He said:

A man and his family had been fishermen all their lives. One day he and his son went out to sea. At first all seemed well; but somewhere along the way, a storm came up. He tried to return to shore before the storm became too severe, but his light was knocked out on the boat by the wind. By now it was pitch-dark because of the storm clouds, even though it was early afternoon. As they fought the waves in an attempt to reach safety, he began to pray.

Meanwhile, his wife (at home) decided to start dinner early because of the storm. She went to the kitchen stove to prepare the meal. After laying the kindling and materials for the fire, she struck a match. It exploded in her hand and caught the oil that was nearby. Suddenly, there was an uncontrollable fire that totally destroyed their home. Knowing that everything was lost, she went down to the docks to wait for her husband and son's return.

When she saw her husband, she began screaming and crying. As she sobbed, she told him the tragedy of their lost home. He quieted her and reassured her that everything was okay. He then said, "We were out in the midst of the sea when a terrible storm arose and knocked out our light. Don't you see? It was the firelight from the house that guided us to safety.

"Thank God you are all right, and thank God our son is safe. We can always build another home; but if not for the fire we would have been lost at sea, and that would have been the end for us."

How do we equate the loss of a home with answered prayer? It was the light from the fire that became the beacon of hope. Although disaster is not the final authority of Christ in our lives, it is often the tool that teaches us to trust in God. Several of the contributors to this book are open and vulnerable regarding the fires that led them to safety in Christ. We are confident that as you review your own struggles in the light of a fresh perspective on prayer and spiritual warfare, what you read here will become a beacon of hope in your life. This kind of power in prayer reminds us that no matter our circumstances, we can depend on God to answer.

Although this book is written from an African-American perspective, it is also written to all believers who desire to see God move among every ethnic group within the inner city. Whatever your background, your ethnicity or your cultural heritage, *our prayer is that you will be encouraged by these testimonies and teachings.*

Rev. Mark Pollard
Atlanta, Georgia
January 2000

Acknowledgments

My mission is to glorify God, the Father, to honor Jesus Christ and extend the ministry of the Holy Spirit as I utilize all my God-given gifts to fulfill my destiny. This book is a testament to God's grace, mercy and loving-kindness. Thank you, Lord.

A special word of thanks and deep gratitude goes to my mother, Ms. Maggie Perry, who prayed for me through every season of life and continues to pray for me.

Without question the stabilizing force in my life next to my walk with Christ has been the rich relationship I've enjoyed with Ella, my wife of 18 years. Thanks for always encouraging, supporting and standing in agreement with one of God's unique ones. Warm regards to my children Daryl, Wesley and Candace. You are my motivation, inspiration and my number-one prayer partners.

A word of honor goes to my special friends, mentors and role models: Dr. R. R. Sommerville, Dr. Verley Sangster, Bishop George McKinney, Dr. William Augustus Jones, Dr. Otis Moss, Rev. J. Langston Boyd, Dr. J. Oswald Sanders, Dr. Walter Brueggeman. And to that great cloud of witnesses—the late Mr. John Wesley Perry, Mr. James Pollard, Dr. Howard Thurman, Mr. James Weldon Johnson, Mr. A. Philip Randolph, Rev. Tom Skinner, Rev. William Seymour, Mr. Marcus Garvey and Dr. Martin Luther King, Jr.

To my colleagues at Common Ground: Bishop Victor Smith, Dr. Bernard Clay, Rev. Kay Ward, Mr. Stan Conley, Mr. Lee Jones and Ms. Marion Smith. What a team! Your partnership in ministry is a source of delight and abundant blessings—let's keep on marching toward the Promised Land!

I am indebted to the Regal/Gospel Light Team: Mr. Bill Greig III, Mr. Kyle Duncan, Mr. David Webb, Ms. Kim Bangs, Mr. Ron Durham and Ms. Deena Davis. You provided constructive counsel without being pushy or critical. Thanks for your empowering style, kind spirit, genuine support and godly patience as we sought to complete this important project in the midst of a hectic travel schedule and many pressing demands. God bless you.

We often presume to know where and how God will advance the vision He has given us. But quite often we are surprised by how and through whom God chooses to do that. We're thankful for the emerging friendship and partnership with Mike and Cindy Jacobs of Generals of Intercession. Thanks for being there for Ella and me, as cheerleaders and networkers.

My ministry and family owe a debt of gratitude to my intercessory prayer team—you know who you are; keep on praying, keep on praising, and keep on prospering.

To the writing team: Dr. Maria Copeland, Revs. Eddie and Mary Edwards, Dr. Clarence Walker, Rev. Ed Barron, Dr. Jerome McNeil, Jr., Dr. Carison Adams, Dr. Walter Fletcher, Pastor Charles Doolittle, evangelist Georgia Ellis, Pastor Joe Thompson and Pastor Donn Thomas—you worked hard, wrote with excellence and waited awhile; so let's spread the word to all we see that *it's prayer time!*

Chapter One

RECONCILING AND RENEWING THE CHURCH THROUGH A NEW MOVEMENT OF PRAYER AND SPIRITUAL WARFARE

Rev. Mark Pollard *is president of the National Common Ground Coalition, an ecumenical ministry located in Atlanta, Georgia, that networks and equips Christian leadership to collaborate in programs and campaigns that spiritually empower African-Americans, people of color and communities of need. He speaks nationally and internationally to a variety of church, political and corporate leaders.*

British author Charles Dickens begins his classic novel *A Tale of Two Cities* with these words: "It was the best of times, it was the worst of times." Obviously, Mr. Dickens was describing the perplexing yet promising conditions of his native England; but this simple phrase is timeless in its irony and transcends mere chronological time.

The phrase appears also to describe modern America, the plight of the African-American and the unique conditions currently facing urban communities. It is the best of times: By all accounts, the black middle class in America is larger and more influential than in the past, and it continues to grow. Yet it is the worst of times: A large proportion of the race seems trapped in the shackles of poverty as the underclass suffer and strain to survive. The best and worst seem linked in some strange sociological joke. For despite the valiant efforts by the civil rights movement to level the political and economic playing field and broker new visions for our empowerment, the majority of African-Americans still struggle to attain the basics of the American Dream.

A Call to Prayer and Fasting

Like the people in Dickens's day, and like many African-Americans today, the disciples of Jesus were also perplexed over the contradictions facing them during their special discipleship training program unit on dealing with evil influences. A man approached Jesus with great urgency, saying that his son suffered seizures that violently flung him into fire or into water. Although the man begged our Lord's disciples to heal his son, they could not. Matthew then says:

> And Jesus rebuked the demon, and it came out of him; and the child was cured from that very hour. Then the disciples came to Jesus privately and said, "Why could we not cast it out?" So Jesus said to them, "Because of your

unbelief. . . . However, this kind does not go out except
by prayer and fasting" (Matt. 17:18-20,21).

The African-American Christians associated with this new
movement to accelerate prayer, fasting and spiritual warfare—of
which this book is a part—are working out of the sense of urgency
implied by Christ when He confronted the enemy. We are fully
aware that the problems we face stem from the work of Satan
himself, and we are fully confident that prayer and fasting offer
the key to overcoming seemingly impossible spiritual challenges.

We raise a rallying cry, a call to arms, a wake-up call to the
Church at large but particularly to the Hamitic stream of the
Church in America—to African-American Christians.[1] Our
prayer is that God would use these resources as a catalyst to
amplify the place of prayer and spiritual warfare within the
African-American church and community. We are hopeful that
in conjunction with a corresponding effort to cooperate with
the broader prayer movement, this will accelerate revival and reconciliation in our families, communities and cities.

The disciples found themselves in a helpless condition when
they tried to perform this miracle of healing and deliverance.
Because their futile efforts were the result of faithlessness, Jesus'
words to them were a form of rebuke, not merely an admonition.
Christ's aim was to forge through necessity a new level of commitment in the lives of the disciples; this book has a similar aim.

Prayer and Covenant Relationship

Jesus' call to prayer and fasting has a rich background extend-
ing all the way back to father Abraham. When Abraham was 99
years old and God appeared to him to enter a covenantal relationship with him, the first thing Abraham did was to fall on
his face in prayer. Prayer and fasting are therefore not works of

human righteousness to pry out blessings from an unwilling God; they are a divinely natural response to God's covenantal blessings. It is only through faith in the God of the Covenant that prayer "works." We cannot even take the first initiative in prayer or arise from our knees to serve others in love without this covenantal God moving us. As Emil Brunner wrote: "Humanity can only be loved from God and unto God. In God Himself is love. . . . Only in the love of God can man be loving, and therefore be himself."[2]

Perhaps the noted author C. S. Lewis said it best in his classic work *Mere Christianity*:

> An ordinary Christian kneels down to say his prayers. He is trying to be in touch with God. But if he is a Christian he knows that what is prompting him to pray is also God. God, so to speak, inside him. But he also knows all that is real knowledge of God comes through Christ, the Man who was God—that is standing beside him, helping to pray for him.[3]

In this context I define prayer as a commitment to respond to or initiate and maintain a consistent divine exchange with the Master. I see fasting as the willingness to submit to higher purposes by sacrificing the mundane for the meaningful.

Thus, many major miracles in Scripture came about as the result of God's people engaged in intentional and steadfast prayer. Most notable are some of the persons who left on record their testimony of faith and fasting: Esther called a fast when her people were in peril, and triumphed over the evil plot planned by Haman; Daniel's commitment to God in prayer brought about his condemnation to the lions' den. Unwavering in faith, he was delivered by God from harm.

And when Jesus came, the bedrock of His ministry was His emphasis on prayer and obedience. He insisted also that those who would bear His name were to reflect this conviction. Jesus prayed before every task and miracle He performed, teaching us the reality and necessity of prayer.

Prayer and the African-American Destiny

Because Jesus addressed the disciples as a group when they asked about the resources available to them to deal with the demonic (see Matt. 17:18-21), I would suggest that an underlying inference here clearly relates to the power of united, or group, prayer. We see a direct connection between Christ's admonition to the disciples in Matthew 17:21 and the call to pray that we are issuing to African-Americans as a group. Our vision is that five years from now the intercessory prayer group will be as popular and numerous in black churches as the gospel choir. Imagine city-wide prayer rallies in our urban centers that are as commonplace as local gospel concerts!

> OUR VISION IS THAT FIVE YEARS FROM NOW THE INTERCESSORY PRAYER GROUP WILL BE AS POPULAR AND NUMEROUS IN BLACK CHURCHES AS THE GOSPEL CHOIR.

The time has come for the emergence of people of color to ascend to the next level of Kingdom leadership. This is so critical to the purposes of God for the Church and our culture that after serving in a fruitful ministry with several parachurch evan-

gelical organizations as a national ministry executive I recon-
nected with The National Common Ground Coalition, an
African-American-led parachurch ecumenical agency, to pursue
this vision. This exciting renewal of global spiritual ambas-
sadorship among persons of African descent is destined to bring
balance to the Church's biblical and prophetic equilibrium.

When my son was about seven years old, we were browsing
in a Christian bookstore. He looked about at the myriad titles
and the pictures of their authors, and after a while he looked up
at me and said, "Daddy, why don't any of these people that write
books look like you?" Of course there are many African-
American authors, but we were certainly underrepresented in
that setting! Even at the tender age of seven, my son felt the
emotional violence done to black people by sheer omission—to
any degree commensurate with their numbers—in countless
frameworks of American life.

African-Americans can therefore serve as chosen instruments
in the hand of God, not only leading a movement of prayer and
fasting but also swinging the nation's moral and spiritual pendu-
lum back to the task of amplifying the call to "do justice," as God
counseled through the prophets (e.g., see Hosea 6:8). It is our
prayer that our efforts will accelerate the work of persons of
African descent in continuing their unique task of restoring the
spiritual luster to a truncated and homogenized gospel. The con-
temporary Church has minimized the biblical gospel to little
more than a hollow industry of evangelical triumphalism and slo-
ganeering. (I will explore this issue in more detail in my upcoming
book called *Higher Calling: Restoring Righteousness and Justice*.)

To fulfill this task will require leaders who are committed
to prayer and fasting: men and women of God who are willing to
sacrifice for higher purposes and maintain a consistent divine
exchange with the Lord.

Celebrating Our Legacy

A great part of making this journey is simply celebrating the richness of our legacy. This call to prayer is more of a plea and vision for a new movement of prayer than it is an indictment on the lack of prayer in the black church and community.

On the contrary, studies show that African-Americans are more likely to attend church regularly than any other racial group, as well as to give a larger percentage of their income to religious and charitable causes, including, of course, the local church. Certainly these qualities of spiritual acumen are the signs of a praying people.

If there is anything black Christians can do well, we can certainly pray and praise! Our elders prayed us through slavery, prayed us through the Jim Crow era, prayed us through lynchings, prayed us through segregation and are praying us through the current civil rights backlash. There is no question that we knew how to pray to overcome.

What is the nature of prayer and spiritual warfare from a distinctive African-African perspective? The answer to this question is threefold.

A MAJOR AFRICAN-AMERICAN DISTINCTIVE IS THE CAPACITY TO OVERCOME SUFFERING AND RESISTANCE THROUGH COMMUNION WITH GOD.

Power to Overcome in the Crucible of Suffering

First of all, I believe that a major African-American distinctive for prayer and spiritual warfare is *the capacity to overcome suffering and resistance through spiritual power obtained in communion with God.*

This supernatural power has been perfected through our experience in the crucible of struggle, pain and suffering. You can hear this theme echoing through this book: overcoming racist scholarship . . . overcoming racist stereotypes . . . overcoming division . . . overcoming pain . . . overcoming personal wounds. There is no question that our elders knew how to pray to overcome. Consider this classic prayer by Zora Neale Hurston, spoken in the cultural lexicon of that era:

> You have been with me from the earliest rocking of my
>   cradle up until this present moment.
> You know our hearts, our Father,
> And all de range of our deceitful minds.
> And if you find anything like sin lurking
> In and around our hearts,
> Ah ast you, my Father, and my wonder-workin' God,
> To pluck it out
> And cast it into de sea of fuhgitfulness,
> Where it will never rise to harm us in dis world
> Nor condemn us in de judgment.
> You heard me when Ah laid in hell's dark door
>   with no weapon in my hand
>   and no God in my heart,
> And cried for three long days and nights.
> You heard me, Lawd,
> And stooped so low
> And snatched me from the hell
> Of eternal death and damnation.
> You cut loose my stammering tongue;
> You established my feet on de rock of salvation
> And yo' voice was heard in rumblin' judgment.
> I thank Thee that my last night's sleepin' couch

Was not my coolin' board
And my cover
Was not my windin' sheet.
Speak to de sinner-man and bless 'im.
Touch all those
Who have been down to de doors of degradation.
Ketch de man dat's layin' in danger of consumin' fire;
And, Lawd,
When Ah kin pray no mo',
When Ah done drunk down de last cup of sorrow,
Look on me, yo' weak servant who feels de least of all.
'Point my soul a restin' place
    where Ah kin set down and praise yo' name forever
Is my prayer for Jesus' sake.
Amen and thank God.[4]

For African-Americans, then, prayer and spiritual warfare is about the connection we have to a God who empowers us to overcome. This awesome God is able to save and deliver us, as evidenced by what He has brought us through. We must revive again the spirit of prayer that undergirded the rallies, the marches and the campaigns during the '60s. We are also challenged to renew the passion to rally together in mass meetings of prayer and singing against injustice and to God's glory. I hear the Spirit calling us anew, wooing us to restore this spirit of the overcomer back to the community. *It's prayer time!*

Bridge Builders and Warriors Against Despair

Bishop Desmond Tutu, the spiritual elder of the South African freedom movement, has stated, "There is no future without forgiveness." As the offended party in a long history of oppressive treatment, the role of African-Americans in the reconciliation movement is central as we are called to incarnate God's love by forgiving and redeeming our oppressors. This was so aptly demonstrated by the loving and nurturing nature of the black maternal figure who cared for the children of white families even while also coping with the indignities and injustices faced as a black person in America.

This suggests the second distinctive of prayer and spiritual warfare from the African-American perspective. It includes the task of *equipping bridge builders and spiritual warriors to challenge both personal and social manifestations of evil and despair.*

Bridge builders are leaders who are gifted at creating change by connecting diverse elements and groups. Spiritual warriors are skilled at winning battles through the implementation of sound strategies. These are descriptions that fit our elders and the leaders of this emerging movement. Several of our key leaders often reference biblical accounts of Nimrod and Hiram, known as *mighty warriors* and *builders.* African-Americans helped to build this country and were essentially forced to fight for every advance and gain currently enjoyed by the black community. As Dr. Clarence Walker poignantly suggests, Satan has sought to corrupt the gift of the warrior within the African-American community, as demonstrated by the startling gang violence, street crimes, domestic abuse and leadership tensions that continue to haunt our community. God is calling us to regain our redeemed fighting spirit to deal a fatal blow to the multiple challenges seeking to level us.

From the African-American Christian perspective, civil rights and social justice are not merely political issues; they are also the natural outgrowth of a life of prayer and fasting. The closer we get to God's heart, the more compassion we gain for others.

Doing justice, caring for the needy, resisting oppressive policies—this is conducting spiritual warfare at the highest level! We bind the strong men of hatred, division and oppression as we pray and fast. Remember, prayer and spiritual warfare are more than personal piety; they are an assault on the evil in our culture and within us.

Spiritual warfare in urban settings includes the task of rebuilding cities and strengthening our roles as prayer-centered fathers, pastors and leaders. It is also about dealing with spiritual wickedness in high places, seeking to loose the scourge of death on the psyche, the spirit and the bodies of black persons, both figuratively and literally.

Assassinating our hope is a strategic weapon in the arsenal of the evil one. Dr. Cornel West affirms this in his book *Race Matters*:

> The proper starting point for the crucial debate about the prospects for Black America is an examination of the nihilism that increasingly pervades black communities. Nihilism is to be understood here not as a philosophic doctrine; it is rather more the lived experience of coping with a life of horrifying meaninglessness, hopelessness, and lovelessness.[5]

Restoring Spirituality to the Culture

African people and their relatives throughout the Diaspora are also called to model spirituality and faith in a world focused on science, logic and technology. Just as Jesus said, "This kind does not go out except by prayer and fasting" (Matt. 17:21, *NASB*), so the potentially demonic and dehumanizing elements of science and technology will ironically be overcome only by a spiritual approach. This leads us to the third distinctive task of prayer and spiritual warfare from the African-American experience: *to bring near the glory and presence of God through tangible experiences and mature lifestyles of spirituality.*

Those churches that take this mission seriously are the churches that are growing most in urban communities. An entire new vanguard of church leadership is emerging from within or alongside denominational groups, and among a whole host of independent church groups. Many dismiss the growth and rise of these ministries as mere examples of shrewd marketing. I beg to differ. These ministries are making a difference and renewing the Church because they are seeking to bring God near in tangible ways.

Leaders like Bishop John Bryant in the AME Church, Dr. Henry Delaney in the CME Church and Bishop Eddie Long in the Baptist church are impacting the Church through such an emphasis. The impact of Bishop Carlton Pearson and Bishop T. D. Jakes cannot be underestimated in this regard as well, particularly but not exclusively among independent churches.

This principle is also why urban praise and worship has become so widespread—it is the fulfillment of God's call on persons of African descent to bring God near. Worship and renewal are spiritual warfare concerns.

Uniting in Prayer

The questions we must face as we advance this new movement are many: What is the state of our relationships across denominational lines? How can we unite to empower hurting people and communities and move beyond our preoccupation with securing the signatures of financial success we have so glibly accepted as signs of God's blessings? How can we rekindle a movement of urgent corporate citywide prayer led by African-Americans? How can we create new institutional and programmatic emphases and roles that will expedite a greater prayer focus within our churches and organizations? Is this next generation of church leadership committed to carrying the mantle of ecumenical outreach and social change to the next level?

Like Nehemiah, who mobilized his community, I have preached for some time now that one of the greatest needs of the black church is to maximize our effectiveness through greater unity. But in recent years it has become increasingly clear that this elusive spirit of unity and the answer to these crucial questions will tarry until we humble ourselves and join together in corporate prayer. This would model a new paradigm for cooperation that moves us beyond the typical political or crisis-oriented gatherings on a national and local level.

We must reconnect as the Hamitic stream of the Church to take care of many pressing family business issues and to overcome our own intrarace breaches in need of repair. Our effectiveness as cross-cultural reconcilers is directly related to our health and security within our own cultural family. Certainly in the Church community we have a long way to go, although without question we are seeing the Lord accelerating the spirit of reconciliation within the Church and society. But prayer and fasting will be required to bring this spirit to fruition.

As a national speaker and ecumenical ministry leader, I have the privilege of networking on a broad national perspective to help increase the spiritual unity of our community and to improve relations cross-culturally between black and white Christian leadership. Recently, in an effort to assess the state of national, corporate and citywide prayer led by African-Americans, I began the process of seeking information on black prayer ministries.

After searching for several months I was able to tap into a rich reservoir of African-American pastors, prayer leaders, intercessors and prophetic leaders who were committed to prayer and spiritual warfare from several denominational backgrounds. I was excited about this new group of leaders but frustrated that except for one

Colorado-based regional network there were no interdenominational prayer organizations or campaigns led by black leaders that connected these key leaders on a formal basis nationally. Contrast this with the host of predominantly white evangelical and charismatic groups centered around prayer, including the National Prayer Committee, Concerts of Prayer, Pray USA, the US Spiritual Warfare Network and Intercessors International, to name a few.

After participating in a series of conference calls, seven of these leaders united in prayer and dialogue to launch the National Council of Urban Prayer Leaders and Intercessors (UPLINC). From these humble beginnings the network now has more than 77 members serving on a national steering committee. There is representation from the AME Church, AME Zion, CME, Church of God in Christ, Church of Christ Holiness, National Baptist Church and Full Gospel Baptist Church, Evangelical Lutheran Church and several independent evangelical and charismatic fellowships. This book project was initiated after the council decided to affiliate with the Common Ground Movement and develop a reconciliation alliance with the US Spiritual Warfare Network.

The council is planning its first National Prayer and Spiritual Warfare Conference, organizing state- and citywide steering committees, and will convene an African-American Gate Keepers Prayer Summit that will lead to citywide prayer rallies the following year. God, indeed, is moving to unite, reconcile and renew the Church!

Personal Pilgrimage Perspectives

Part of the vision of this movement and this book, with their appeal for an acceleration of prayer and spiritual warfare among black churches, lies in two very personal experiences I must share with you. These events have both shaken me and made me more keenly aware of my own need for deeper consecration, and have increased my confidence that God is calling for renewed awareness of the power of prayer.

The Cost of Ignoring God's Voice

An experience in Memphis, Tennessee, several years ago resensitized me to the reality of spiritual warfare on a personal basis. Although I have pastored for several years, planted churches and launched and overseen numerous urban ministry and youth efforts, a growing intensity in my ministry in the areas of racial reconciliation and social justice exposed me to new levels of spiritual resistance and battles that I had never before encountered. I believe these attacks were in direct proportion to the significance of my mission of helping to restore a vision of righteousness and justice to the Church and the nation.

I was scheduled to go to a conference in Memphis, dealing with such issues. As I made my plans to attend, I became aware of a definite word from the Lord that I should not go. In my own mind, however, I was certain that it was important for me to attend the conference. I was scheduled to speak, and I had several significant appointments lined up; so in spite of the strong impression that it was not the Lord's will that I go, I went anyway.

A ministry associate attended the conference with me and we visited the Civil Rights Museum, which is on the site where Martin Luther King, Jr., was assassinated. It was a quite moving experience, seeing displayed the story of the civil rights movement from the Jim Crow era to the present liberation movement. After our tour, we left the museum and headed back to the church where I was to speak that afternoon.

About the time that we arrived at the church, I began to feel dizzy and felt a swelling in my chest and some shortness of breath. I went into the restroom, and in the mirror I noticed that my upper lip had swollen to twice its normal size and that my neck was extremely swollen, too. I left the bathroom in shock, and a staff person sent for a nurse. She was extremely concerned that there might be internal swelling in my chest and throat, which could mean that I might choke to death if I didn't get to the hospital immediately.

My associate took me to the Methodist Hospital, where doctors saw me immediately. They were concerned about an allergic reaction and asked me questions about my diet—whether I had eaten certain nuts or seafood—not knowing that I had been fasting and praying for several days leading up to the conference. They gave me medicine that they said usually reduced the swelling within an hour. But an hour later the swelling was worse.

I did not want to alarm my wife, but I wanted her to know my condition, so my associate called her. In turn, my wife called about seven of our intercessors to pray about my condition. Meanwhile, another injection failed to reduce the swelling. About that time my wife called back with the report that the intercessors had identified my ailment as a spiritual attack from the enemy, something apparently related to the legacy of Memphis. They committed to continue in prayer but were certain that breakthrough and healing were nearby. We were encouraged by their exhortation, though interestingly their final words were that I should leave the city as soon as I could.

What was amazing was that 30 minutes later the doctors essentially said the same thing—that I should leave Memphis—apparently feeling that I was allergic to something in the atmosphere. Incredible! My partners in prayer had already spiritually tapped into what the doctors' diagnosis turned out to be. This experience once again confirmed the wisdom of having an intimate group of intercessors consistently covering me in prayer and available for crises like this one.

Not long after I left Memphis to return to Atlanta, the swelling finally went down. Glory to God! The power of prayer prevailed on my behalf. All this left me convinced that I had taken too lightly the level of spiritual warfare the enemy was willing to wage against the work I was doing.

About this time I learned that a former associate with whom I had worked in youth ministry had died from what seemed to be a similar attack, confirming my conviction that we were engaged in spiritual warfare. From that moment on, I have taken to another level in my life the importance of both spiritual warfare and of being obedient to the Lord after consulting Him for His will in my life on a daily basis.

My Prayer Partner and Mentor, "Dad" Mason

A second personal experience involves my prayer-partner relationship with Dr. Elliott Mason, Pastor Emeritus of Trinity Baptist Church in Los Angeles. This wonderful man of God, almost 80 years old, sometimes affectionately called "Dad" Mason by a few, admitted to me that after all his years in dynamic ministry—including 300 conversions a year, healings, prayer crusades and the like—*he still was learning how to pray.*

"What do you mean?" I asked. And as he articulated it, I realized he was talking about a dimension of prayer that I too was lacking in: the part that involves not just talking to God in structured prayer times but also *listening* to God wherever we are. We can increase our capacity to hear the Lord clearly as we're driving across town, speaking to non-Christians and otherwise involved in activities we usually consider to be outside of our "prayer closets" and private devotional regimens.

So it was Dr. Mason who deeply impacted my spiritual life, particularly in the arena of prayer and contemplation. He also influenced my definition and understanding of prayer as a *rela-*

tionship with God that involves both speaking and responding to Him in every activity of life.

For example, I remember asking Dad Mason what he thought of helping me with an important project, and he replied, "I can't even talk about that yet until I talk to the Lord about it." Though he loved me and was committed to assisting me any way he could, he always made it clear, without offending me, who the Boss was and who it was he was afraid of offending. That was again an indication of how this precious man of God, who has been a model, mentor, pastor and successful leader for so many years, was still committed to interacting with God at such a deep level.

Dr. Mason not only models success as a leader, but more importantly he also models humility that was birthed out of his life of prayer and an ever-growing intimacy in his relationship with God. As we pray together over the telephone and as I pray with the many young leaders God has allowed me to mentor, I am continuing to learn that listening to God is half the battle of prayer. It is out of that growing awareness, rather than the feeling that I have "arrived," that I have answered God's call to mobilize and unite others to the task of confronting the evil forces that come against us and to advance the Kingdom through united prayer power.

Our God is able. The strongholds that have frustrated God's people are falling down. Yes, indeed, *it's prayer time.*

Notes

1. According to Genesis 10:6, Ham's descendants were Cush (the biblical name for Ethiopia), Mizraim (Egypt, including the upper and lower Nile), Put (Libya and possibly Punt, an old kingdom that straddled the Red Sea) and Canaan (which the Israelites later conquered). Later in the Bible, the word "Ham" more narrowly designated Egypt (see Psalms 78:51; 105:23,27; 106:22). However, the use of "Ham" in this place follows the popular custom of associating Ham with black Africa and black Africa alone.

2. Emil Brunner, *Man in Revolt* (New York: Scribner's, 1939), p. 219.

3. C. S. Lewis, *Mere Christianity* (New York: Macmillan Company, 1960), n.p.

4. Zora Neale Hurston (1891-1960) was a writer during the Harlem Renaissance (1920-1930) and an expert in African-American folklore. Internet: http://lowelg.simplnet.com/Prayer. htm

5. Dr. Cornel West, *Race Matters* (New York: Knopf, 1994), p. 22.

Chapter Two

LORD, TEACH US TO PRAY

Dr. Maria-Alma Rainey Copeland *is the former pastor of Mizpah Lutheran Church in St. Louis, Missouri, and director of Peace Ministries in Salisbury, North Carolina.*

And it came to pass, that, as he was praying in a certain place,
when he ceased, one of his disciples said unto him,
Lord, teach us to pray, as John also taught his disciples.
Luke 11:1, *KJV*

Prayer is essential. It is the bedrock for the People of God. In our pluralistic society where anything goes, prayer continues to be the ingredient that stabilizes our faith in God. The Old Testament contains evidence that prayer is interacting with God, and Jesus gave the example for us to follow: We must pray. The Gospel of Luke records several accounts of Jesus in prayer.

Whatever the disciples had observed when Jesus was praying, created a desire within them to know how to do the same. Therefore, they said to Him, "Lord, teach us to pray."

Frank Laubach, founder of the Laubach Literacy Program (used worldwide), wrote that "prayer is the mightiest force in the world. Desperately eager people would pray if they knew that prayer can save the world. They are waiting for us to lead the way."[1]

When I was growing up in North Carolina, my mother taught us to begin our days with prayer. She and the other women in our community always got up before 6:00 A.M. for prayer. Since I was the oldest of four children, she would awaken me. "You have to get up before Satan," she would say. Now, at age 88, she continues to get up to pray before 6:00 A.M., even though the other ladies have now been called from the Church Militant to the Church Triumphant and gone on to glory.

We grew up in an African-American neighborhood typical of those often scathingly referred to as the "ghetto." Ghetto or not, it was the only home we had. Prayer was effective in this neighborhood. One of the most amazing phenomena of this community was that in spite of the low socioeconomic status of the families, most of the children were either college graduates or college educated. Fewer than 10 of the youth had an encounter with the police, and none was ever incarcerated. In retrospect, we witnessed the words of the Scripture: "The prayer of a righteous [person] has great power in its effects" (Jas. 5:16, *RSV*).

During my childhood we would hear our grandparents talk about praying. They always said, "If *Jesus* had to pray, what about you and me?" As they were praying, they always included this line in their prayers: "Lord, search my heart, my mind, my thoughts, and don't let anything get between You and me, separating me from Your gracious love and source of power." I am not sure that I fully understood what they were saying then, but maturity has given me a better understanding. It is out of my experience as a child who grew up with family prayer as a daily ritual that this chapter is written.

The Power of Persistent Prayer

Prayer is more than repetitive monotones. It is a form of praise, thanksgiving, adoration and intercession. It has great power and potential.

The Scriptures teach us to be persistent in prayer—we are to "Pray without ceasing" (1 Thess. 5:17, *KJV*). It is important that we maintain a *daily* prayer life. What we pray for in secret, God answers openly. Prayer can reach where we can only imagine, going into places where we can't go or be at the time we are praying; and it will do things we cannot see. It will change not only conditions but the hearts of humankind as well.

The question has been asked, "Why pray at all if God already knows what we are going to say?" We pray because we want to be in obedience to God's Word. This is His plan for our lives as we communicate with Him.

We have God's promise that He will hear and answer our prayers: "Call upon Me in the day of trouble; I will deliver you" (Ps. 50:15). Then, too, Christ taught us to "Ask, and it will be given to you. . . . For everyone who asks receives" (Matt. 7:7,8).

Martin Luther wrote regarding prayer:

It is quite true that the kind of babbling and bellowing that used to pass for prayers in the church was not really prayer. To pray as the Second Commandment teaches us is to call on God in every need. This God requires of us; He has not left it to our choice.[2]

Jesus' Format for Prayer

The Gospel writers Matthew and Luke were very precise in teaching us the formula that was included in the Disciples' Prayer, often called the Lord's Prayer. When His disciples asked, "Lord, teach us to pray," Jesus designed a format with such precision and innocence that it has come down through generations without being tampered with. Within this prayer is everything we need.

Some years ago, during our first assignment to Germany, one of the ladies in our weekly Bible class passed out an outline of the Lord's Prayer. We were not told where she got it; we simply copied what she gave us. It helped us to better understand Jesus' format for prayer. There were 23 topics to define its real meaning; consequently, whenever we use it, everything that is needed is included. The following are the topics and the respective corresponding phrases from Matthew 6:9-13 (*KJV*):

Relationship—"Our Father"
Recognition—"Which art in heaven"
Adoration—"Hallowed be thy name"
Anticipation—"Thy kingdom come"
Consecration—"Thy will be done"
Universality—"In earth"
Conformity—"As it is in heaven"
Supplication—"Give us"
Definiteness—"This day"
Necessity—"Our daily bread"
Penitence—"And forgive us"
Obligation—"Our debts"
Forgiveness—"As we forgive"
Love and Mercy—"Our debtors"

Guidance—"And lead us"
Protection—"Not into temptation"
Salvation—"But deliver us"
Righteousness—"From evil"
Faith—"For thine is the kingdom"
Humility—"And the power"
Reverence—"And the glory"
Timelessness—"For ever"
Affirmation—"Amen"

From catechism we had learned that this prayer contains seven petitions and the doxology, which helped us to understand better what was being said.

Unfortunately there are frequent objections to praying this prayer because some have become disgruntled over its recitation. But it is my strong belief that there is power in this prayer. And we may well ask objectors why they are intimidated by it if they believe there is nothing to it. Their distress is an affirmation that the prayer is effective. At any rate, in this day and age, no other exercise or behavior has been more criticized or scrutinized than prayer.

What Is Prayer?

This question—what is prayer?—has been asked many times over the years and has some very simple answers. Prayer is entering into communication with God—coming face-to-face with God.

Prayer is not hocus-pocus, mumble-jumble magic words. It is entering into conversation with God. The Old Testament records the earliest instances of prayer: the conversation between Adam and God—the first encounter between God and humankind after man had deliberately disobeyed God. "Then the LORD God called to Adam and said to him, 'Where are you?' So he said, 'I heard Your voice in the garden, and I was afraid because I was naked; and I hid myself'" (Gen. 3:9,10).

Adam's son Cain also talked with God after God had asked him about his brother Abel. Cain complained to God about his punishment. He said to the Lord, "My punishment is greater than I can bear!" (Gen. 4:13).

The story of communication between God and man continued when God spoke to Noah regarding His wrath upon the earth—sending the flood. The first use of the word "covenant" appears here as God makes an agreement with Noah and his sons: "But I will establish My covenant with you; and you shall go into the ark—you, your sons, your wife, and your sons' wives with you" (Gen. 6:18).

After Moses had been called to lead the Children of Israel out of Egypt, the Scriptures teach that he too spoke face-to-face with God: "Thus the LORD used to speak to Moses face to face, as a man speaks to his friend" (Exod. 33:11, *RSV*). Moses' relationship with God was one of continual communication with Him. Moses' dependence upon God is seen throughout the narrative history of Israel under his leadership.

Prayer Conforms Us to God's Will

Prayer is more than a pious ceremony or formality. Offered with sincerity, faith and truth, prayer has a transforming effect on our lives.

The disciples had watched Jesus praying on various occasions. The inner circle—Peter, James and John—were the three disciples who had accompanied Jesus when He went up on the mountain to pray. Luke says that "as He prayed, the appearance of His face was altered, and His robe became white and glistening" (Luke 9:29). Through prayer, Jesus was transformed on the mountain as He appeared with Moses and Elijah. Although the disciples didn't have the full understanding of what this meant, they knew that prayer was important.

PRAYER DOES NOT ALWAYS RESULT IN SOMETHING INSTANTANEOUS OR SENSATIONAL. IT IS A LIFE-FORMING EXPERIENCE THAT ENABLES US TO IDENTIFY THE WILL OF GOD FOR OUR LIVES.

God will also transform us through prayer. It does not always result in something instantaneous or sensational, making headlines in the evening news or on the psychic hotlines, nor is it the latest fad to be paraded at every juncture of life. Rather, prayer is a life-forming experience, the height of spiritual communion with God, enabling us to identify the will of God for our lives.

In the garden of Gethsemane shortly before His death, Jesus was in agony as He prayed:

> Sit here while I pray. . . . He said to them, "My soul is exceedingly sorrowful, even to death. Stay here and watch." He went a little farther, and fell on the ground, and prayed that if it were possible, the hour might pass from Him (Mark 14:32,34,35).

God's purpose for His only begotten Son was death on Calvary to redeem humankind back to Him. As Jesus prayed, He was able to overcome His agony and pray into the perfect will of

God. That is why during His time of prayer He was able to say what can be considered one of the most powerful statements in human history: "Nevertheless, not what I will, but what You will" (Mark 14:36). This is why, in His high-priestly prayer, Jesus could later say to the Father, "I have manifested Your name to the men whom You have given Me out of the world" (John 17:6).

The prophet Jonah had to deal with a similar problem of the will. He had been instructed to go to Nineveh to proclaim God's word of salvation and hope to this city-state. However, he was determined at first to do his will instead of God's will, violating God's purpose for his life. He was so reluctant to go to Nineveh that he boarded a ship bound for a different destination. When the storm arose, Jonah was tossed into the sea and a fish swallowed him. Even then he wasn't convinced that he should go to Nineveh.

> Now the LORD had prepared a great fish to swallow Jonah. And Jonah was in the belly of the fish three days and three nights. Then Jonah prayed to the LORD his God from the fish's belly. And he said, "I cried out to the LORD because of my affliction, and He answered me. Out of the belly of Sheol I cried, and You heard my voice (Jon. 1:17–2:2).

Unfortunately, after God's merciful interaction with Jonah, he became angry with God because the people of Nineveh repented when they heard God's Word, and God extended His mercy toward them and didn't destroy the city at that time. Likewise, we often become upset because God doesn't answer our prayer in accordance with the way we have prayed it. God answers prayer according to His will: "'For My thoughts are not your thoughts, nor are your ways My ways,' says the LORD" (Isa. 55:8).

Like Jonah, we foolishly allow feelings to override faith. Former U.S. Army chaplain Merlin Carothers wrote in his book *Power in Praise*:

> Jesus said, "Pray in faith, believing you have received." We can't pray the prayer of faith if we insist on measuring the results by our feelings. We may discover that God's truth in the Bible often says we should do the exact opposite of what we feel. "Love your enemies," said Jesus. Doesn't he know how we feel about our enemies? Sure He does. But He is telling us that we don't let our feelings boss us around anymore. We are free to choose to love even our enemies![3]

Prayer is essential in order to be obedient to God's Word instead of following our own feelings. Prayer is not answered according to the will of humanity but according to the will of God. The apostle Paul summed up his experience in these words:

> And to keep me from being too elated by the abundance of revelations, a thorn was given me in the flesh, a messenger of Satan, to harass me, to keep me from being too elated. Three times I besought the Lord about this, that it should leave me; but He said to me, "My grace is sufficient for you, for my power is made perfect in weakness" (2 Cor. 12:7-9, *RSV*).

The Unlimited Power of Prayer

The regular Wednesday-night Bible study on "The Power of Prayer" was filled with excitement. The most pressing question asked was, What could we ask God and expect to receive? At the end of the session, one of the young ladies addressed the group. She said, "Pastor, will you pray for me to have a son? My doctors have told me that I am a high-risk person, and they have little hope for a safe delivery." The women in the class sighed with empathy and told her that we would pray. Using Mark 11:24— "Therefore I say to you, whatever things you ask when you pray, believe that you receive them, and you will have them"—we surrounded her and began to pray. Using the process of laying on of hands as a point of contact, we made our request known.

It was four months later during another Bible-study session that our sister told us with joy that the doctors had confirmed her pregnancy. She said she would keep us updated on her condition. We did not cease to pray for her. Later we were told that she was carrying a boy. We rejoiced, for this is what we had prayed for. At the end of her term, she gave birth to a healthy baby boy who was baptized six weeks later.

We had believed the words of the psalmist who wrote, "Delight yourself also in the LORD, and He shall give you the desires of your heart. Commit your way to the Lord, trust also in Him, and He shall bring it to pass" (Ps. 37:4,5). We shared her joy when the Lord fulfilled this promise. At the same time, we knew that God does not answer our every whim or desire. It is not our responsibility to determine what prayer He will or will not answer.

One of the ladies told us that she had prayed for more than one child. However, her prayer was never answered. She told us of her pain and desire. Somewhere along the way, her faith was strengthened. She learned to live with her disappointment. Years later, the doctors discovered that her blood had an Rh-negative factor. She had been blessed to have one live birth, while her other pregnancies had ended in miscarriages. She told us that she had asked God why and that she felt so inadequate. "I can understand why the women of the Bible felt that they had been reproached by God when they were barren," she said. "But now I have learned to trust God and I know that it is in His will to do all things."

That ladies' Wednesday-night Bible-study group had some amusing answers to prayer as well. This was a military ladies' group. The army base where we were stationed allowed the families to remain behind while the military members were overseas. We began to pray, "God, bless our group to continue to grow"—but we didn't specify *how* we wanted it to grow, we simply prayed for increase. God chose to answer our prayer by allowing eight of the ladies to give birth, all within months of each other!

One of the ladies conceived after 15 years, and when it was time for the delivery, she asked for the group's help. We had come in from our usual walk when the telephone rang. She was on the phone asking for prayer because she was going through very painful labor contractions. Again, members of our ladies' group, which was also a prayer chain, were contacted and we began to intercede for her, asking God for deliverance from her pain. She called from the hospital a couple of hours later, telling us that God had blessed her with an eight-pound four-ounce baby girl. We rejoiced with the new mother (see Phil. 4:4). We were jubilant with praise; God had answered our prayer.

Prayer knows no barriers or boundaries. Our hope in God's mercy to do great things comes from our experience and relationship with Him. We can utter our whole desire to Him. Out of our walk of faith, our hearts become enlarged and concerned for the welfare of others. In his book *Touch the World Through Prayer,* Pastor Wesley Duewel writes:

Prayer can transcend "the laws of nature." Prayer can bring God's miracle answers to man's desperate needs. It would be useless to pray for many problem situations if this were not true. If there are limits to what God can do when we pray, then prayer is playing games with God, trifling with human need, and deceiving ourselves. Prayer is as real as God is real. . . . Prayer releases God's power.[4]

Of course, everyone who prays knows that not all our prayers are answered in the way we ask. There have been many instances to cause me to ponder long and intensely in prayer. Why are some prayers answered and others are not? My father's illness made me take a long look at that question. We had been praying for my father's healing from cancer. We listened to many testimonies of God's healing and knew of some cases as well. Nevertheless, our prayer for my father did not result in one of those healing stories, and he died. It became very difficult to accept the words of Scripture: "Rejoice always, pray constantly, give thanks in all circumstances; for this is the will of God in Christ Jesus for you" (1 Thess. 5:16-18, *RSV*).

That passage of Scripture seemed to be totally out of line with human reality. The pain of losing my father was too intense. Only through fasting and prayer was I enabled to come to terms with my dad's death.

Ironically, I had been a pastor for a number of years. Somehow, this didn't make too much difference. This was a new type of pain. Out of that experience I learned a great lesson: *Faith in God is not dependent upon whether or not our request in prayer is answered in the positive. The form of God's answers will never negate His ability to answer them.*

Intercessory Prayer and God's Will

Often the vicissitudes of life leave us too weak to pray for ourselves, so we are taught to pray for one another. This is intercessory prayer—praying on behalf of individuals or nations.

In His Own Way

A telephone call informed me that one of my parishioners was in the hospital with only a 15 percent chance of survival. She had just given birth to a baby son, and everything had gone wrong. Her life was hanging by a thread. Although her mother was a member of the church, I didn't know this lady. She had been baptized in the church where I was pastor, but she had never attended during the first five years of my pastorate. My experience as hospital chaplain alerted me to the immediacy of the matter. Responding to the call, I discovered that her condition was critical, as the chaplain had said. In order to go into the room, which was a sterile area, I had to be masked, gowned and gloved.

When we saw her after consulting with her doctors, we knew she was in serious trouble. We knew also that our only hope was prayer. Prayer partners were contacted and we began to pray around the clock. Some weeks later, she was moved from her isolated area to a less restricted one. Her condition improved, allowing her to go home a few months later. To this date, she has not committed her life to Christ; nevertheless we were made aware of the power of praying for others. And it was another lesson for me about when and how God chooses to answer prayer.

It is a blessing to be in Christ, but we can't demand that He answer our prayers our way. We can only trust in His mercy and His faithfulness as we pray for one another. As Paul said, "I urge that supplications, prayers, intercessions, and thanksgivings be made for all men" (1 Tim. 2:1, *RSV*).

God answers intercessory prayers—but always in His own way.

Arguing on Behalf of Others

In the Old Testament, intercessory and even argumentative prayers were offered to God by Abraham, Moses and the prophets. The earliest recollection of intercessory prayer was when God decided to destroy the cities of Sodom and Gomorrah. The wickedness of the people had become intolerable, and God shared His plans with Abraham:

> Because the outcry against Sodom and Gomorrah is great, and because their sin is very grave, I will go down now and see whether they have done altogether according to the outcry against it that has come to Me; and if not, I will know (Gen. 18:20,21).

When Abraham learned that God was considering destroying Sodom, where his nephew Lot lived, he began to plead with God on behalf of the city. "Would You also destroy the righteous with the wicked? Suppose there were fifty righteous within the city; would You also destroy the place and not spare it for the fifty righteous that were in it?" (vv. 23,24).

Here intercessory prayer begins in earnest. Abraham emptied himself before the Lord and poured out his soul in prayer for a city whose wickedness had brought the wrath of God down upon it in judgment. Abraham asked God not to be angry with him because of his persistence in prayer for Sodom. He did not plead for himself or his house. Except for his nephew, Lot, and his family, he had no personal stake in these cities. To continue to plead on their behalf meant taking on the responsibility of intercessory prayer for cities that were already doomed. His friendship with God empowered him to plead in a desperate situation. His faith in God never wavered even in the hopelessness of the situation.

And Abraham prevailed! God knew the condition of these cities, but He knew Abraham as well; and He promised not to destroy the city if there were as many as 10 righteous persons there (v. 32).

Moses Prays for Israel

Another example of intercessory prayer comes from Moses' encounter with God on behalf of Israel. God was angry when the people made the golden calf and worshiped it, so He threatened to disown Israel. He said to Moses:

> Go, get down! For your people whom you brought out of the land of Egypt have corrupted themselves. They have turned aside quickly out of the way which I commanded them. They have made themselves a molded calf, and worshiped it and sacrificed to it, and said, "This is your god" (Exod. 32:7,8).

But Moses interceded on the people's behalf, pleading with God to spare them because His enemies would say that He had taken Israel out of Egypt just to destroy them. Moses reminded God of His promise to Abraham, Isaac and Israel (Jacob). God heard Moses' plea on behalf of Israel: "So the LORD relented from the harm which He said He would do to His people" (v. 14).

Daniel Intercedes for Israel

The prophet Daniel also interceded on behalf of the people in captivity. Although He was aware of the gravity of Israel's sins, he prayed that God would "hear the prayer of Your servant, and his supplication. . . . For we do not present our supplications before You because of our righteous deeds, but because of Your great mercies" (Dan. 9:17,18).

Daniel fasted and prayed for 21 days. God let him know that He had heard his prayer when it was first prayed and encouraged him, saying, "O man greatly beloved, fear not! Peace be to you; be strong, yes, be strong!" (10:19).

The words spoken to Daniel are a reminder to all of us not to become discouraged when our prayers are not answered according to our timetable. Daniel's prayers are reminiscent of intercessory prayers we should offer on behalf of America. Here is a country that has forgotten where God has brought us from. We are a nation that has always bombed other countries, while our land has been spared. There are vigilante groups in the land who think they can set off a bomb whenever and wherever it pleases them, but this is not like having to run for shelter when the sirens sound. Remembering the drills of World War II and the blackouts is enough to call us to pray for our nation. We pray, remembering God's words to Solomon:

> If My people who are called by My name will humble themselves, and pray and seek My face, and turn from their wicked ways, then I will hear from heaven, and will forgive their sin and heal their land (2 Chron. 7:14).

This is a call to become involved in intercessory prayer on both a personal and a national level.

Unknown Intercessors

One of the most meaningful metaphors of intercession comes out of the airports across the country. Each plane that takes off or lands is in the hands of a pilot who is so high up in the cockpit that he is unable to see immediately below the plane. Therefore a "ramp master" must "stand in the gap" to guide the pilot to safety.

This ramp master is an inconspicuous person with two flares, one in each hand. He or she must use the flares in order to direct the planes. These persons don't command a lot of attention. The acclaim is reserved for the pilots and flight attendants walking through the terminal. Most of the time, ramp masters won't get a second glance. Nevertheless, they have one of the most important jobs at the terminal.

It is the same way with intercessory prayer. Most persons involved in intercessory prayer will never make the evening news or the headlines for being steadfast in prayer. Nevertheless, what they achieve in prayer is more than we'll ever know.

Praying According to His Will

One of my most difficult experiences in prayer is the test of praying according to God's will. Once I was praying about a very personal matter. Each time I tried to say, "If this is not Your will for my life, Lord, then I don't want it." But I felt as though a hand was squeezing my heart. Needless to say, I didn't finish the prayer. But I didn't stop agonizing about it. Finally, after three days of fasting, I was able to empty myself before God and *mean* it when I told Him that if this was not His will, then I didn't want any part of it.

I was learning something about surrendering my will to God's will, just as in Jesus' prayer in the garden of Gethsemane. He was able to say, "Not My will, but Yours, be done," but only after He had prayed, "Father, if it is Your will, take this cup away from Me" (Luke 22:42). At first, Jesus expressed His own desire; then He surrendered to God's desire.

The Importance of Humility

We cannot pray to God with a haughty spirit, demanding that our prayers be answered. Instead, we come to God in humility and contrition, with the understanding that we are dependent upon His mercy and grace. The prophet Isaiah wrote, "I dwell in the high and holy place, with him who has a contrite and humble spirit, to revive the spirit of the humble, and to revive the heart of the contrite ones" (Isa. 57:15).

We had been invited to the presidential inauguration in Washington. This was a time of great anticipation. The festivities had begun with a breakfast reception in our representative's office in the Rayburn Building. We were given tickets to both the swearing-in ceremony and the luncheon immediately following. When we received the tickets, a quick glance indicated that they were color coded, with specific areas designated to sit or stand. Moments after leaving for the ceremony, I discovered that my ticket was different from the others. It never occurred to me that I would be separated from the group. By the time we were in place, thousands of persons had arrived, totally separating me from my group and leaving me isolated and on my own.

When the ceremony was over, I had no idea which way to go to find my group or the way back to my hotel. The crowd immense, and somehow I was just carried along. Believe me, I was humbled! But rather than panic, I began to pray. These words from Proverbs came to mind: "Trust in the LORD with all your heart, and do not rely on your own insight. In all your ways acknowledge him, and he will make straight your paths" (3:5,6, RSV).

I knew this was not a time for me to rely on my own wisdom. I prayed, "Jesus, I am lost. I don't know where I am, but You do. Help me to find a cab so that I may return to my hotel safely and in time for the parade." Shortly thereafter, I looked into the faces of two ladies who were smiling. I introduced myself and explained my plight and asked for directions. One of the ladies suggested I could use the Washington metro system. Of course this was met with a blank stare and the words, "Where do you get it? I am not from this area."

With my reply there came more detailed instructions and directions. Then, abruptly, one of the ladies said, "Never mind, I'm going that way." As we walked along in conversation, I discovered that she was a missionary and deeply involved in the work of evangelism. We soon discovered that it was impossible to obtain a cab. The area was filled with limousines. They had literally choked out the taxicab waiting area. This sight filled me with a sense of panic and fear. I was alone in the crowd, virtually lost. I began to pray again and was reassured with the words, "For He shall give His angels charge over you, to keep you in all your ways" (Ps. 91:11).

As if sensing my fear, my companion said, "Come, I will take you on the Metro with me. You can get off at your stop and walk to your hotel. It's not very far." Then she added, "No! On second thought, I will go with you; then I will know that you are safe and I won't have to worry about whether you arrived there or not." My heart filled with gladness. We arrived at my hotel with minutes to spare. The lady stayed with me during a 45-minute wait and then said, "Now I can leave you, for I know that you are safe." With that she seemed to vanish in the crowd.

Later, I tried unsuccessfully to reach her at the telephone number she gave me. I never saw her again, even though I looked as far as I could in the crowd after I had been cleared to find my seat. I had made my request known to God and He had answered me. As the apostle John assures us:

> Now this is the confidence that we have in Him, that if we ask anything according to His will, He hears us. And if we know that He hears us, whatever we ask, we know that we have the petitions that we have asked of Him (1 John 5:14,15).

Prayer and the Search for a Center

Prayer has a centering effect upon our lives. There is a difference between being *self-centered* and having a *centered self.* Through the Holy Spirit we can have an *inner* relationship as well as an *inter-*relationship with God; and it is prayer that brings this inner relationship into balance with Him, as well as with our entire being. As Cecelia Bryant writes in *I Dance with God*:

> Our spirituality is a part of our body, mind, feelings and will. It is a part of our worship, work, play and rest. As God seeks to be always and everywhere present, so we seek to be always and everywhere present to God. Prayer is centering our lives in our relationship with God in Christ and allowing the center to be present in all we do.[5]

This centeredness is aided by praying in the Name of Jesus, and by the work of the Holy Spirit. Jesus promised His disciples to send the Holy Spirit—the Comforter—who is our guide and teacher and who would remind us of the things that He taught. One of the things He taught was that we should pray in His Name. From that center, we move outward and inward—outward into the mainstream of life and inward in His will. Paul wrote to the Romans:

> Likewise the Spirit helps us in our weakness; for we do not know how to pray as we ought, but the Spirit himself intercedes for us with sighs too deep for words. And he who searches the hearts of men knows what is the mind of the Spirit (Rom. 8:26,27, *RSV*).

Christ is our center. When we cease to pray, we sever the connection with Him and cut off the source of power that comes to us from God through and by the Holy Spirit.

It is important during our prayers that we ask God to search our hearts, our minds and our thoughts so that we do not allow anything to get between us, thereby separating us from the source of His power; we want no obstacle to hinder our prayers from being answered.

When God Seems Silent

Many people become confused when their prayers do not result in the triumph of what they perceive to be the good. Even at such times, we can find refuge in knowing that God's will and His way are not our ways: "'For My thoughts are not your thoughts, nor are your ways My ways,' says the LORD" (Isa. 55:8).

At the close of Bible study, one of the ladies told us that her coworker had asked her a question she wasn't sure how to answer: "Where was God during slavery and all of its cruelty?" Her question stymied most of us, and we gave it a lot of thought before any of us tried to answer.

The question made me think of the many painful and horrible stories of slavery that my great-great-grandmother and grandmother told us when we were growing up. Our great-great-grandmother was a slave and was sold and separated from her family. Through prayer, God blessed her mother to be sold to the same person who had bought her children. We grew up knowing these stories, and I myself had prayed for answers to questions similar to the one sought by the woman at our Bible study.

Finally, I answered her: "God was where He has always been—here and throughout the world, heaven and earth. Because of sin, God has suffered many things to happen, even allowing His Son to be crucified by sinful humankind. Sin is at the core. But even during slavery, God never ceased to be God." During our discussion, someone repeated a statement from a cab driver who told her, "If I didn't believe in the power of prayer, I wouldn't pray."

Certainly our nation has felt the results of the evils of slavery. "Righteousness exalts a nation, but sin is a reproach to any people" (Prov. 14:34). Slavery left many generations with questions, but God has not forgotten His world or His peoples. Israel was under Egyptian bondage for more than 400 years. In all of that time God was not silent, and He is not silent now. Believers have been told that we are a royal priesthood and a holy nation (see 1 Pet. 2:9). We are "heirs of God and joint heirs with Christ" (Rom. 8:17). Just as Christ intercedes for us, we can do the same for the nations that practice evil. Isaiah had this to say of the Messiah: "He bore the sin of many, and made intercession for the transgressors" (Isa. 53:12).

As the Body of Christ, we are called to be intercessors. There are conditions and persons that we need to intercede for. In worship service, each time we sing the Kyrie we chant the prayer, "In peace let us pray to the Lord"; and we respond, "Kyrie Eleison, Lord have mercy." We conclude our petitions with "Lord, in Your mercy, hear our prayer." [6]

Steadfastness in Supplication

Jesus taught that we "always ought to pray and not lose heart" (Luke 18:1). The term "supplication" implies that kind of constancy in prayer. Paul counseled us this way: "Be anxious for nothing, but in everything by prayer and supplication, with thanksgiving, let your requests be made known to God" (Phil. 4:6).

A few years ago, the theme for the church year was "Rooted in Prayer." It is important that we live in a constant attitude of prayer. By doing so, we remain in fellowship with God and His will. When we walk constantly with the Lord, we are impressed with *His* constancy. Living in an attitude of supplication empowers us to say, "Father, thank You for everything—my trials and tribulations as well as my blessings." In the midst of it all, God is still there enabling us to endure.

ONLY WHEN WE LEARN HOW TO NAME OUR PAIN AND ACKNOWLEDGE OUR TRUE FEELINGS TO GOD CAN WE BE HEALED. YET, WE TOO OFTEN PRAY ONLY FOR IMMEDIATE RELEASE.

Years ago, I experienced a devastating hurt I thought I would never get over. Once, as I was pouring my heart out to God, I suddenly felt an overwhelming sense of rage. I was on the verge of saying, "I hate the source of my pain!" when the image of the Cross loomed before me. Seemingly, all I could hear were these words: *Are you justified in hating?* With those words, I began to sob, "God, I hurt!"

Years later, I realized that I needed to remain in a spirit of supplication long enough and intensely enough to identify my pain in order to allow God's healing grace to deliver me from it. Only when we are patient enough to learn how to name our pain and acknowledge our true feelings to God can we be healed. Yet even though we know that strength comes through adversity, we too often pray only for immediate release.

When I was a pastor in Ohio, I assisted at a revival at one of our sister churches. Each night we were praying for long lines of worshipers. The bulk of the requests were along the lines of "Pray for me that I may grow strong." Many of the requests seemed to lack sincerity. They did not indicate a willingness for patience in supplication.

Persistent supplication brings results. Jesus told a parable about a widow and an unjust judge. The woman came to the judge every day, asking him to vindicate her against her adversary. Finally, the judge said, "Because this widow troubles me I will avenge her, lest by her continual coming she weary me" (Luke 18:5).

An experience I had in the New Mexico desert helped me to understand the importance of persistent supplication. I had to make a daily journey of 105 miles round-trip from El Paso, Texas, to Las Cruces, New Mexico. One day I had just turned off the highway onto a desert road when my car began losing speed.

I tried downshifting the gears, but that didn't help; and finally my car rolled to a complete stop. Another motorist who had been behind me pulled up and told me that my car was smoking. I knew I was in trouble when the car wouldn't start. The driver offered me a ride to the nearest station, 10 miles away, where I called my husband. I was confronted with the dilemma of what to do with the car. If I left it where it was, I could be cited for abandoning an out-of-state automobile, and thieves would strip it clean. I began to pray.

When my husband arrived, he couldn't get the car started either. We were in trouble, and I began to pray in earnest. Nothing seemed to happen. Three times I prayed, remembering the story of Elijah when he prayed for rain. Soon after I finished praying the third time, a wrecker went right past us. My heart dropped. I remembered the words of Psalm 18:6 and prayed more: "In my distress I called upon the LORD, and cried out to my God." Immediately the wrecker turned around and came back. The driver told us that he would take the car with him to the city where he was going and then bring it back to us in El Paso.

When he told us that he lived two blocks away from us in El Paso and would only charge for the distance from his house to our residence, I knew that God had worked a miracle for us. If we had been charged the regular fee, it would have been more than we could afford. God had supplied an answer to my supplication.

"Whatever You Ask"

We have been given divine *carte blanche* when we pray: "Whatever you ask in My name, that I will do, that the Father may be glorified in the Son. If you ask anything in My name, I will do it" (John 14:13,14).

No other person or source can make this declaration. The promise is accessible by faith, through which we recognize not only the value of prayer but of God Himself. We can call on Him anytime and at any place.

When the disciples asked Jesus to teach them to pray, He looked down through generations of hardened sinners, on into our own times, and He saw our need to learn to pray as well. He saw that men and women would become so wicked that they would openly defy God and seek to change His plan for their lives. He designed prayer so that He could take care of all our needs.

All we have to do is pray. And those who long to pray acceptably still make the supplication, "Lord, teach us to pray!"

Notes

1. Frank Laubach, *Prayer: The Mightiest Force in the World* (Grand Rapids, Mich.: Fleming H. Revell, 1946), p. 46.
2. Edward M. Plass, *What Luther Says* (Saint Louis, Mo.: Concordia Publishing House, 1997), p. 1056.
3. Merlin R. Carothers, *Power in Praise,* ed. Jorunn Oftedal Ricketts (Plainfield, N.J.: Logos International, 1972), p. 34.
4. Wesley Duewel, *Touch the World Through Prayer* (Grand Rapids, Mich.: Zondervan Publishers, 1986), p. 25.
5. Cecelia Bryant, *I Dance with God: A Cojourney in Prayer* (Dallas, Tex.: Akosua Visions, 1995), p. 18.
6. *With One Voice: A Lutheran Resource for Worship* (Minneapolis: Augsburg Fortress, 1995), p. 28.

Chapter Three

CONFRONTING CRITICAL ISSUES FACING OUR COMMUNITY

Rev. Mary Edwards *is founder of the Joyful Heart Ministries and a popular conference speaker.* **Rev. Eddie Edwards** *is president of Joy of Jesus, a nationally recognized Christian community-development ministry.*

For generations, the roots of racism and inferiority have oppressed the African-American people. These spirits took root from various myths, not the least of which is the diabolical lie that we are a cursed people because we are descendants of Ham. Many of us have bought this lie and see ourselves as "grasshoppers" rather than descendants of kings, queens, educators, inventors, writers and other people of great worth.

This chapter will detail how the lie got started, who told the lie, how it has negatively impacted the African-American people, and then address who we *really* are and how to undo the lie. The axe must be laid to the roots of racism and inferiority in order for us to be able to enter into our full destiny.

The axe is prayer!

Before we can discuss any of the above, however, it is important first to set the stage for our commentary. Even though the primary audience consists of members of the Body of Christ, we do not want to overlook the opportunity to stress the importance of the spiritual development of *all* people.

This is especially relevant because some of our remarks will be global in nature, applying to anyone who wants to see God's kingdom come on earth, as well as to those who want to enter therein.

The Kingdom of God

Any immigrant from a foreign country coming to the United States of America, must meet criteria for entering the country. Likewise, there are conditions for entering the kingdom of God. Not everyone will enter (see Matt. 7:21-23). So what is the kingdom of God, and what are the criteria for becoming a citizen?

First, Scripture tells us that the kingdom of God is not merely in word but also in power (see 1 Cor. 4:20). In other words, it's not in our talk alone but, more importantly, in our walk. The power is in our walk in Christ.

Many words have been and still are being spoken that have hurt African-Americans as a people. Some of these will be discussed later in this chapter. The Bible tells us that the letter kills, but the Spirit maketh alive (see 2 Cor. 3:6). Words can kill, but they can also heal. Our prayer is that our words will bring healing to the reader.

Second, the kingdom of God is a place where God the Father has sovereign rule and reign. It is a place where He alone governs and has dominion. He's the King who sits on the throne. There is none higher in authority than the King of Glory. The kingdom of God is a place where every knee bows and every tongue confesses that He is Lord (see Isa. 45:23; Phil. 2:10,11).

Conditions for entering the kingdom of God begin with the new birth. Jesus said, "Most assuredly, I say to you, unless one is born again, he cannot see the kingdom of God" (John 3:3). Other conditions include humility (see Matt. 18:3), sympathetic service to others (see Matt. 25:31-46), perseverance (see Col. 1:22,23; Heb. 3:14), faith (see Heb. 4:14) and love (see Gal. 5:6).

What we are speaking about here is the content of one's character. Character is the inward condition of one's heart that dictates a person's walk and his talk. That's why Jesus said to the disciples in Luke 17:21 that "the kingdom of God is within you."

The importance of our character can be further supported when we look at the fruit of the Spirit (see Gal. 5:22,23) and the Beatitudes (see Matt. 5:3-11). Don't for one moment think that you can exhibit the fruit of the Spirit or live up to the Beatitudes in your own strength. It takes God's power to fulfill these criteria. The power of God is His Holy Spirit, our enabler (see Acts 1:8). It is the Holy Spirit who, among other activities, enables us to live a righteous life.

Righteousness is more than good behavior. Righteousness is doing God's will for your life with the right motives, in God's way. Righteousness exalts a nation (see Prov. 14:34). Righteousness involves right standing with God and right standing with one another. Jesus Christ is our righteousness (see 1 Cor. 1:30). Without Him, we can do nothing (see John 15:6).

Without Him, we cannot keep the new commandment that Jesus gave us, which is to love one another (see John 13:34,35). When Jesus said "Love one another as I have loved you," He didn't mean for us to love only those in our own race but everyone in all races. Past history, as well as current events, has proven time and again that we haven't even loved those within our own race. African-Americans have not only been enslaved by European slave owners; they have also enslaved one another.

It is probable that Nimrod, a black man (being a descendant of Cush), could not have built his eight great ancient cites (see Gen. 10:8-12) without recourse to slave labor.[1] This means that as long as 4,600 years ago our own people may already have been selling us to slave traders. We are still enslaving ourselves for drugs, guns, money and material goods, fame, fortune and power. Black-on-black crime can be seen in every community across our nation and even in our families. Fathers against sons. Mothers against daughters. Brothers against sisters. Husbands against wives. Division within our very own families.

The greatest tragedy of all is that we have enslaved ourselves. We have sold ourselves into slavery to others because we have lacked a knowledge of our own rich heritage. We have listened to and believed that we are who others say we are, instead of discovering for ourselves who we really are. As a result of buying racist lies, a spirit of inferiority has taken root in our hearts. We must lay the axe to the root. Let's put the lies on the chopping block!

Roots of Satan's Strategy

Ever since Lucifer lost his place in the kingdom of God, he has done everything within his limited power to tear God's kingdom down. Four of his most effective tools have been deception, discouragement, division and disobedience.

For generations, Satan, the father of lies, has given birth to lying seeds. It began in the Garden of Eden when Eve told God that "the serpent deceived me, and I ate" (Gen. 3:13). What has often been referred to as original sin led to disobedience and division, two of Satan's other strategies.

One of the many deceptions, and one that has done great destruction to African-American people and caused division among ourselves, is the strategy Satan used in stirring up British slave owner William Lynch against our people.

The Curse of Willie Lynch

In 1712, the slave owner Willie Lynch—from whom we get the term "lynching"—was invited to the Colony of Virginia to teach his evil methods to slave owners in the United States. Following is the satanic speech he gave to his American cohorts:

> Gentlemen, I greet you here on the bank of the James River in the year of Our Lord one thousand seven hundred and twelve. First, I shall thank you, The Gentlemen of the Colony of Virginia, for bringing me here. I am here to help you solve some of your problems with slaves. Your invitation reached me on my modest plantation in the West Indies where I have experimented with some of the newest and still the oldest methods for control of slaves. Ancient Rome would envy us if my program is implemented. As our boat sailed south on the James River, named for our illustrious King, whose version of the Bible we cherish, I saw enough to know that your problem is not unique. While Rome used cords of wood as crosses for standing human bodies along its old high-

ways in great numbers, you are here using the tree and rope on occasion.

I caught the whiff of a dead slave hanging from a tree a couple of miles back. You are not only losing valuable stock by hangings, you are having uprisings, slaves are running away, your crops are sometimes left in the fields too long for maximum profit, you suffer occasional fires, your animals are killed, gentlemen, you know what your problems are; I do not need to elaborate. I am not here to enumerate your problems, I am here to introduce you to a method of solving them.

In my bag here, I have a fool proof method for controlling Black Slaves. I guarantee everyone of you that if installed correctly, it would control the slaves for at least 300 years. My method is simple and members of your family or your Overseer can use it.

I have outlined a number of difference(s) among the slaves; and I take these differences and make them bigger. I use fear, distrust, and envy for control purposes. These methods have worked on my modest plantation in the West Indies and will work throughout the South. Take this simple little list of differences, think about them. On top of my list is "Age," but it is there only because it starts with an "A." The second is "Color" or "Shade," there is intelligence, size, sex, size of plantations, status on plantation, attitude of owner, whether the slaves live in the valley, on a hill, East, West, North, or South, have a fine or coarse hair, or is tall or short. Now that you have a list of differences, I shall give you an outline of action but before that, I shall assure you that distrust is stronger than trust and envy is stronger than adulation, respect and admiration.

The Black Slave, after receiving this indoctrination, shall carry on and will become self-refueling and self-generating for hundreds of years, maybe thousands.

Don't forget you must pitch the old black versus the young black male and the young black male against the old black male. You must use the dark skin slave vs. the light skin slaves and the light skin slaves vs. the dark skin slaves. You must also have your white servants and overseers distrust all Blacks, but it is necessary that your slaves trust and depend on us. They must love, respect and trust only us.

Gentlemen, these Kits are keys to control, use them. Have your wives and children use them, never miss an opportunity. My plan is guaranteed and the good thing about this plan is that if used intensely for one year the slaves themselves will remain perpetually distrustful.

Thank you, gentlemen.[2]

Willie Lynch's strategy has contributed greatly to the roots of racism, division and inferiority, which have been embedded in the hearts of our people for centuries.

The Curse of Ham

Unfortunately, the roots of Satan's lies go back even further than Willie Lynch. So get ready for a black history lesson. Let's begin with the controversial "curse of Ham."

After researching what various Bible scholars had to say about this topic, we want to thank Pastor Jefferson Edwards for what we consider to be the clearest narrative on this issue. Pastor Edwards is the founder and pastor of Inner-City Christian Center in Kansas City, Missouri. He feels a special commission and calling to bring down the barriers that divide races and denominations. We appreciate Pastor Edwards's treatment of this issue, and we use his book *Chosen, Not Cursed* as the source of the following explanation of the curse of Ham:

> The entire land of Canaan was inhabited by dark-skinned people. Canaan and Cush were sons of Ham. Ham was the father of the dark-skinned race, and the black race evolved through his son, Cush. Ham means "hot," or "dark, colored or swarthy."
>
> The Hebrew word for Ham [means] "hot," and is prophetic of the climates that have created the blackness of skin of the Negro and the dark complexions of other people from the same stock.
>
> Egypt is called, "the land of Ham" (Ps. 105:23). The Egyptian word for *Ham* means, "black and warm." From Ham we have the Egyptians, Africans, Babylonians, Philistines and Canaanites. The land of Canaan, which was promised to Israel, was a land of dark-skinned inhabitants.
>
> When Israel inhabited the land of Canaan, it was fulfillment of the curse pronounced on Canaan by Noah. In fact, there is a controversial issue that relates to what is called "the curse of Ham."
>
> Many teachers, secular and religious, have said that blacks are in the lower levels of society and continue to be an oppressed faction because they are under the "curse of Ham" to be "servants."
>
> This is another lie from Satan that justifies oppression and continues to perpetuate racism. The curse was on Canaan, not Ham. "And [Noah] said, 'Cursed be *Canaan*; a servant of servants he shall be to his brethren' " (Gen. 9:25). The indignation of Noah found expression in the thrice-repeated curse upon *Canaan* (see Gen. 9:25-27).

The truth is that the curse of servitude was fulfilled in Joshua's conquest of the Canaanites and their land when he made them hewers of wood and drawers of water.

> Now therefore ye are cursed, and there shall none of you be freed from being bondmen, and hewers of wood and drawers of water for the house of my God. And Joshua made them that day hewers of wood and drawers of water for the congregation, and for the altar of the Lord, even unto this day, in the place which he should choose (Josh. 9:23,27, *KJV*).

The fact that God gave Israel the land of the Canaanites was a fulfillment of the curse on Canaan to be servants.[3]

When one lives under the systematic scheme of lynchings and under the diabolical lie of the curse of Ham for generations, one can readily understand how the spirits of racism and inferi-

SATAN HAS DONE A THOROUGH JOB OF STEALING OUR HERITAGE AND OF KILLING OUR SPIRITS, SOULS AND BODIES; HE HAS NEARLY DESTROYED AN ENTIRE RACE OF PEOPLE.

ority, and their offspring—deception, discouragement, division and disobedience—have taken root. The content of Satan's character—to steal, kill and destroy (see John 10:10)—has impacted the African-American people for hundreds of years and many generations.

Satan has done a thorough and wicked job of stealing our heritage and of killing our spirits, souls and bodies; and he has done his best to destroy an entire race of people.

An example of how Satan uses people to perpetuate his lies and cause confusion can be found in the book *The Racial Streams of Mankind* by Dr. Clem Davies, a Ku Klux Klan member, pastor and early promoter of the so-called "Christian Identity" movement, who shares ambiguous and racist views of Ham and black people in Scripture.

Even a cursory read of Davies's writings show contradictions. On one hand, he states that "the Hamitic stream" is identified with the African people. But with the next stroke of the pen he states that "Ham was not a colored person." He leaves it for one to assume that if Ham was not a "colored person," then he must have been a white person. If this were true, why would he be the only white person among the dark peoples of the story? Davies doesn't make any effort to explain.[4]

Although Dr. Davies relates Egypt to Ham, he maintains that as the Hamites moved into inner Africa, they became "darker" spiritually, intellectually and physically:

> Thus Ham became the father of the Egyptians, the early Chaldees, and the Canaanites. His descendants journeyed deeply into Africa, and the deeper they went, the less became their wisdom. They became beings between men and brutes; their very souls and brains were different. They were not "men of like passions as we are," and finally even their very dialects—the most meager and monosyllabic of all the original speech were lost. They became ugly and degraded.
>
> You have only to witness the films shown today of the natives of "darkest Africa" to see what depths the

Hamitic strain has descended to an utterable mental and spiritual darkness, the veritable nadir of civilization.[5]

Without a doubt, such misinterpretations of biblical history as they pertain to blacks have contributed greatly to the roots of racism and inferiority.

One final note with regard to the subject of the curse of Ham. Some of the material researched was so disgusting that I had to fight back waves of nausea. At one point, I wrestled with a gigantic headache. Because this is a chapter in a book on prayer, I thought it would be a good idea to stop and pray and ask God what He thinks about all of this. So I did, and God has spoken these words to my heart:

This is not a white issue. Nor is this a black issue. This is a sin issue. I do not curse color. I curse sin. Canaan wasn't cursed because he was black but because the nation of Canaan did wickedness in My sight. The United States of America has also sinned greatly. They have had other gods before Me. They have committed adultery and fornication. Like the land of Canaan, America is also sin-sick. But I have not cursed America. In fact, I have many people in America. And when My people, who are called by My name, shall humble themselves and pray and seek My face and turn from their wicked ways, then will I hear from heaven and will forgive their sin and will heal their land (see 2 Chron. 7:14-16).

With these words in mind, dear friends, let me give you a good report. We have a glorious heritage in the Lord. Let's look further at who we are.

Who We Really Are

The historical truth relating to our ancestry will negate the deception of the enemy that causes us as individuals and as a race to accept racist lies and the spirit of inferiority. God said that His people are destroyed for lack of knowledge (see Hos. 4:6). The information contained herein is a fraction of the documented truth that is now available for us to understand. In all our getting, we must get an understanding of who we are naturally and spiritually in order to fulfill our God-ordained purpose.

THE HISTORICAL TRUTH RELATING TO OUR ANCESTRY WILL NEGATE THE DECEPTION OF THE ENEMY THAT CAUSES US AS INDIVIDUALS AND AS A RACE TO ACCEPT RACIST LIES AND THE SPIRIT OF INFERIORITY.

We owe a debt of gratitude to Raymond H. Woolsey for the excellent research in his book *Men and Women of Color in the Bible*. Woolsey tells us that a black man[6] played a major role in the construction of King Solomon's Temple. This wasn't just an ordinary man; he was Hiram, king of Tyre. Woolsey writes:

> Hiram had been a close friend of David. When the latter was building his palace in Jerusalem, Hiram had supplied cedar from the renowned forests of Lebanon. Now, Solomon made arrangements for more supplies for the building of the Temple. Solomon supplied laborers to work with Hiram's skilled timbermen for the felling of cedar and fir. The logs were floated in great rafts down the seacoast to a spot near Jerusalem and taken overland

to the Temple. Hiram's men—Phoenicians, descendants of Canaan—also worked with Solomon's skilled stonemasons for the preparation of the huge stones that went into the Temple walls. The workmanship was so carefully done at the quarry that when they were put into place in the Temple, not a sound of chisel or hammer [was] heard.[7]

Not only was Hiram a wealthy man in authority, but also his workmen were skilled tradesmen who performed their work with a high standard of excellence.

An overview of the stunning wealth of the Queen of Sheba (Sheba is located in what is now called Yemen) is given in the book *Blacks Who Died for Jesus* by Mark Hyman:

There were 797 hot and tired camels and donkeys in the Queen of Sheba's caravan. They had labored 1,250 miles, carrying maximum loads of heavy gold and other jewelry, woods of numerous kinds, preserved foodstuffs and hundreds of gallons of water picked up along the way. In the center of the caravan was the queen's veiled carriage made of weighty gold and hardwood. She was carried on the shoulders of young male servants.

Over 150 crack troops of the palace guard and the Ethiopian army marched in the royal section with the queen [as well as] thirty or more handmaidens, cooks, beauticians and skilled craftsmen, such as jewelers, leather workers, map readers, chemists, priests, magicians, philosophers, astrologers and other men who knew how to guide the ships of the desert. These "ships" carried twenty million dollars' worth of gifts.[8]

Even today, $20 million is still six (plus) zeros! This queen was a double-digit millionairess. Her jewelry box was filled to the max! She was giving away her overflow.

Even though the Queen of Sheba was unbelievably rich, what she gave was nothing compared to what Jesus wants to give us—life "more abundantly" (John 10:10). God is no respecter of persons (see Acts 10:34). We have all been created in His image (see Gen. 1:27). That means far more than this chapter will allow us to share, even if we fully understood the breadth, length, height and depth of what that means. From a spiritual perspective, however, being created in God's image means that we are joint heirs with Jesus Christ (see Rom. 8:17). We are fearfully and wonderfully made (see Ps. 139:14). And we are royal priests, acceptable and pleasing to God, chosen and precious in His sight (see 1 Pet. 2:4,5).

God's Word tells us that we shall know the truth, and the truth will make us free (see John 8:32). The operative words in this Scripture are "truth" and "make." Truth brings about a spiritual release that we must act upon (make), liberating us from the bondage of the deception we have believed. In the Bible this deception is called walking in darkness. The truth of who we are and the rich heritage we have from our forefathers in Africa also spans the ocean and the desert which our ancestors had to cross as slaves. Only the strongest of the strong survived the cruelties of traveling conditions, the embarrassment of the auction blocks, the plantation system's undignified treatment, the separation of family, the raping of women and the denial of freedom and education. All of this inhuman treatment because of the color of our skin!

When we were emancipated in 1865, we were faced with the challenge to build a nation of people who would be able to make more than a physical contribution to our nation. We were challenged to participate in the creative development of America. Today, less than 140 years after being emancipated, as we move from the Industrial Age to the Information Age, we have come a long way in a very short period of time. This is due to God's presence with us and His leading us to our destiny as a people.

As individuals and as a people, we must embrace God's principles and move ahead as He told Joshua:

> Only be strong and very courageous, that you may observe to do according to all the law which Moses My servant commanded you; do not turn from it to the right hand or to the left, that you may prosper wherever you go. This Book of the Law shall not depart from your mouth, but you shall meditate in it day and night, that you may observe to do according to all that is written in it. For then you will make your way prosperous, and then you will have good success (Josh. 1:7,8).

In addition to this stunning history of royalty and wealth before slavery, the qualities of godliness, intelligence and leadership can also be found in the character of our Midianite ancestors (the Midianites are called black Arabs). This can be seen in the life of Jethro, the father-in-law of Moses (see Exod. 18:18-27).

God had directed Moses to go to Jethro and be taught how to serve. Jethro was a Midianite priest or chief. He was a wise man, and Moses learned under him. Jethro's name actually means "excellency." He had a spirit of excellence in his character. He knew the lay of the land, and Moses wanted him to travel with him and the children of Israel to be their "eyes" as they journeyed through the wilderness toward the Promised Land.

For far too long we've been on the bottom and at the end of the line. But now is the time for us to become spiritual eyes to the Body of Christ. God is giving us strategic insight to lead the Church.

In order for us, as a people, to catch up and be of value in this new Information Age, we must rid ourselves of all the old baggage of lies and stereotypes that have been self-deceptive and divisive. As we walk in the truth of the light that leads us, we will begin to lead the whole nation of America out of darkness. This, I believe, is our destiny as a people. It will give testimony to the world of the power and glory of the living God, as we become a prosperous, loving, forgiving and godly people, full of faith in the living Christ.

Since emancipation from slavery some years ago, the strongest of the strong have struggled to assimilate into American culture. During our darkest period, there was one hope and one hope only: Jesus Christ would deliver us and make us free. This truth is available to us today as individuals and as a nation.

What Can We Do?

As we bring this chapter to a close, we leave you with thoughts and suggestions for laying the axe to the root of racist lies and the spirit of inferiority.

1. Put on the Whole Armor of God

The apostle Paul urges us:

> Finally, my brethren, be strong in the Lord, and in the power of his might. Put on the whole armour of God, that ye may be able to stand against the wiles of the devil. For we wrestle not against flesh and blood, but against principalities, against powers, against the

rulers of the darkness of this world, against spiritual wickedness in high places. . . . Stand therefore, having your loins girt about with truth, and having on the breastplate of righteousness; and your feet shod with the preparation of the gospel of peace; above all, taking the shield of faith, wherewith ye shall be able to quench all the fiery darts of the wicked. And take the helmet of salvation, and the sword of the Spirit, which is the word of God: praying always with all prayer and supplication in the Spirit, and watching thereunto with all perseverance and supplication for all saints (Eph. 6:10-12,14-18, *KJV*).

In this passage, our Lord reveals to us who our enemy is and where he operates. We need to be strong in the Lord's power and put on His full armor so that through Him we will have victory both as *individuals* and as *a people*. We must walk in this armor, applying truth, righteousness, peace, faith, the Word of God and prayer—daily, in all situations.

2. Pray for Your Enemies

Pray a blessing for your persecutors, as Paul commanded in Romans 12:14: "Bless those who persecute you; bless and do not curse." Pray that God, through the Holy Spirit, will help you to love your enemies as our Lord commanded:

Ye have heard that it hath been said, Thou shalt love thy neighbour, and hate thine enemy. But I say unto you, Love your enemies, bless them that curse you, do good to them that hate you, and pray for them which despitefully use you, and persecute you (Matt. 5:43,44, *KJV*).

This is the way of love, which represents the sharpening of the axe.

3. Present Your Body to God

Again, turning to the apostle Paul, in Romans 12:

> I beseech you therefore, brethren, by the mercies of God, that you present your bodies a living sacrifice, holy, acceptable unto God, which is your reasonable service. And do not be conformed to this world, but be transformed by the renewing of your mind, that you may prove what is that good and acceptable and perfect will of God (vv. 1,2).

4. Clean Your House

Before you can do any of the above, there's one very important step you need to take: You must first clean your own house. Ask God to reveal to you any unconfessed sin within your own heart; then repent and ask forgiveness. Then you can bind and cast out, *in Jesus' name*, those ungodly spirits you have identified during your time of reflection and repentance. Following is a suggested prayer:

> Father, I confess as my sin_____*(name sins)*_____.
> I repent and ask for Your forgiveness. In the name of Jesus and by the power of His shed blood on Calvary, I bind_____*(name sins)*_____, cast them out and send them to their appointed place.

After these sins are bound and cast out, be sure to seal the door of your mind and cover it with the precious blood of Jesus so that these spirits cannot reenter.

When you have dealt with your own issues, such as unforgiveness, ungodly thoughts of anger, hatred, bitterness and an attitude of inferiority, then you can bind and cast out evil spirits in your enemies. Remember: Beelzebub cannot cast out Beelzebub (see Matt. 12:25-29). If we are full of hatred ourselves, we cannot cast out the sin of racism in someone else. We must first clean our own houses. After the strong man has left, we can fill the house with an even stronger Man, Jesus Christ!

Notes

1. "The enlistment of forced labor to carry out the building and agricultural programs of the state was common in the ancient Near East. Villagers, resident aliens, and the disenfranchised were the primary target groups for this sort of conscription." K. C. Hanson, "Slavery," *The International Standard Bible Encyclopedia*, ed. Geoffrey W. Bromiley, vol. 4 (Grand Rapids, Mich.: W. B. Eerdmans, 1979), p. 540.
2. "Willie Lynch's Speech on Slave Control," Internet: www.blackspeak.com/speeches/slavecontrol.htm.
3. Jefferson D. Edwards, *Chosen, Not Cursed* (Broken Arrow, Okla.: Vincom Publishing, 1989), pp. 32, 33.
4. Clem Davies, *The Racial Streams of Mankind* (n.p., n.d.), p. 60.
5. Ibid.
6. That Hiram was "black" is inferred from the fact that the Phoenicians, whose main cities included Tyre and Sidon, were relatively dark-skinned Mediterranean peoples.
7. Raymond H. Woolsey, *Men and Women of Color in the Bible* (Langley Park, Md.: International Bible, Inc., 1977), p. 50.
8. Mark Hyman, *Blacks Who Died for Jesus* (Nashville: Winston-Derek Publishers, 1988), p. 70.

Chapter Four

SHATTERING THE STRONGHOLDS THAT HINDER EMPOWERMENT IN THE AFRICAN-AMERICAN COMMUNITY

Dr. Clarence Walker *is a certified marriage and family therapist in private practice in Philadelphia, and the senior pastor of Fresh Anointing Christian Center.*

It is my sincere belief that African-American people and people of color in general will have a significant role in the upcoming revival as well as the final war against the forces of darkness. Black people have always been formidable warriors.

Mighty Black Warriors in History

Let's begin with Nimrod, who was a Cushite (an Ethiopian). Scripture says of him that "Cush was the father of Nimrod, who grew to be a mighty warrior on the earth. He was a mighty hunter before the LORD" (Gen. 10:8,9, *NIV*).

The term "mighty warrior," translated from the Hebrew *gibbor*, means great warrior, conqueror, giant superhero, champion or valiant. No other personality was individually identified in this manner during this period of time.

This black man emerged to be the greatest warrior of his day. Legends about Nimrod say that he was such an awesome fighter that he fought and conquered animal predators with his bare hands. In spite of his faults and subsequent notoriety, he cannot be denied his place in biblical history and history in general. He was the first man mentioned in the Bible as a great warrior.

First Samuel 17:4 mentions another formidable warrior, Goliath of Gath, a Philistine. According to Genesis 10:13, the Philistines were descendants of Ham's second son, Mizraim—an ancient biblical name for Egypt. The name Ham (or Cham) means warm, dark and hot. Therefore, Goliath was a Hamite, a man of color. Prior to his encounter with David and ultimate defeat, no one in the Bible world of that day would deny that the Philistines had a champion, the likes of which there was no equal in size or ability. The same term used of Nimrod, *gibbor*, was used of Goliath (see 1 Sam. 17:51).

Consider also Ishmaiah, a Gibeonite warrior who joined David's military at Ziglag. He soon became a member of David's 30 mighty men (1 Chron. 12:4). The Gibeonites were Canaanite descendants of Ham, a powerful and renowned people who inhabited the city of Gibeon, which also inhabited by Amorites and Hivites, all descendants of Ham. When the pagan king of ancient Jerusalem heard that Gibeon had feared Joshua's conquering forces so much that they sued for peace, he "feared greatly, because Gibeon was a great city, like one of the royal cities, and because it was greater than Ai, and all its men were mighty" (Josh. 10:2).

In Isaiah 18:2, the Bible says that the Ethiopians, or Cushites, who were black, were a people that were "terrible from their beginning." In Hebrew, the word "terrible" means greatly feared and awesome. *The Amplified Bible* says they were "[feared and dreaded near and far], a nation strong and victorious, whose land the rivers divide!"

The children of Ham have gone on to produce some of the greatest warriors in history, including the black soldiers who chased Robert E. Lee in the Civil War, Shaka Zulu of Africa, Queen Nzinga, and boxing warriors such as Joe Louis, Sugar Ray Robinson, Muhammad Ali and Evander Holyfield. Unfortunately, we have not always been on the side of right.

Channeling the Warrior Legacy

We have often been found fighting against God. It has been the goal of Satan to pervert the great-warrior legacy of the Hamitic (black) people by fueling the rage so that we turn on each other. Tribalism in Africa is a classic example of this spiritual perversion. The urban gangs of black youth are nothing more than the stronghold of tribalism manifested among our youth. Think of what could happen to Satan's kingdom if we could convert these black youth and teach them to channel their warrior nature spiritually against the forces of darkness that seek to destroy our people!

I submit to you that spiritual warfare as it relates to the black community must be focused on getting these warriors saved and recruited into the Lord's army. Moreover, we must help those saved black men already in the Church to tap into their rich warrior heritage and transform that energy into spiritual warfare consciousness.

DISUNITY, DIVISIVENESS AND RESISTANCE ARE STRONGHOLDS AMONG BLACK PEOPLE, AND IT IS THESE STRONGHOLDS THAT SHOULD BE A TARGET FOR PRAYER.

We must expose them to Satan's tactics of getting them to fight either God or each other. The adversary will not give up quickly on these tactics because they have worked so well for generations. Disunity, divisiveness and resistance are strongholds among black people, and it is these strongholds that should be a target for prayer. We must strategically focus on those areas that particularly hold African-Americans in bondage.

Toward More Positive Strongholds

Not only were Hamites great warriors, but they also were well known and well versed in another military category: *stronghold builders*. In order to subdue Canaan, Joshua had to defeat 31 Canaanite strongholds. Most of them were well-built fortresses of defense. In other words, black people knew how to make great strongholds.

I believe this is true not only in the natural realm but also in the spiritual realm. We have generationally constructed spiritual strongholds that we feel comfortable defending. What can we learn from Joshua's experience with the Canaanites?

Joshua and Jericho

Consider Jericho, the first stronghold that Joshua and the Israelites faced. It was significant because it was designed to be able to withstand siege warfare. The city was designed with thick walls and a glacis—a steep-angled ramp that was set against the walls—to prevent rolling seige towers and engines of war coming up against them.

Such defenses symbolize the condition of black people who have several generations of people living in the same stronghold. By virtue of our strong multi-generational family networks, we often have three or four generations of blacks bound with the same chains.

Paul mentions the word "stronghold" in 2 Corinthians 10:3-5. The original Greek word is *ochuroma*, meaning "a fortified place of defense, a fortress, castle or [even] a stubborn argument." Spiritually, a stronghold is often erected as a defense against God. It consists of the arguments, reasoning, ideologies, philosophies and rationale that are contrary to and in opposition to the knowledge of Christ. They are against Christ and therefore anti-Christ. Thus, where you find spiritual strongholds you will also find a spirit of anti-Christ.

Jericho was also significant because it was the first and primary stronghold faced by Joshua and his armies. In order to take Canaan, Joshua had to conquer Jericho. Likewise, it is important that we identify the "Jericho," or principal stronghold, among black people—the root of any opposition against God. Once we have taken the primary stronghold, the others are easier. But much time is wasted when we don't identify and go after the main "Jericho."

The third reason Jericho is significant is because of who was laying siege to the fortress and who was inside it. Joshua was the man charged with taking Jericho. His name is the Hebrew equivalent of the Greek name "Jesus." They both mean "Jehovah is salvation" or "Yahweh saves." Therefore, Joshua (Yeshua) is an Old Testament "savior." And in an even more powerful way, the Savior Jesus can defeat the spiritual strongholds that keep black people bound.

Joshua had a dual ethnic nationality. Through his ancestor Ephraim he could trace his lineage to Joseph, who was descended from Shem (see 1 Chron. 7:20-27). Through his ancestor Asenath, Joseph's wife, he could claim Egyptian blood (see Gen. 41:50-52).

Rahab, who lived in Jericho, is the other significant person in the account of the fall of this stronghold. She was a Hamitic Amorite, who was also one of the descendants of Ham. The Amorites were the most Negroid looking of the Canaanites.

Unlike others in Jericho, Rahab feared the true God and desired deliverance. What she needed was somebody like Joshua and his army to break down the walls and defeat the army of Jericho to bring her and her family out to safety (see Josh. 2:1–6:27). Joshua, a Semite with an African bloodline, had to go in and bring out a Hamite woman of African lineage. In order for this to happen, the walls of the stronghold Jericho had to fall.

Strongholds Among Black Men

Among black people there are many "Jericho walls" that have to fall. One of these strongholds is the wall of violence. This bloody-warrior syndrome causes our men to be violent toward each other in crime and in gang warfare, and their wives and children to suffer physical abuse. The number one cause of death of black men between the ages of 15 and 34 is homicide! We are losing our youth warriors at alarming rates. The walls must come down!

The resilient stronghold of drugs relates to our African heritage of witchcraft. This also is a wall that must come down! The Bible lists witchcraft among the works of the flesh in Galatians 5:20 (*KJV, NIV*). The Greek word for "sorcery" and "witchcraft" is *pharmakeia,* from which we get our term "pharmacy," a word that is associated with drugs and medication. It may further be interpreted as illicit or illegal pharmaceutical use of drugs, as in certain magical practices. What we call drug addiction is akin to what the Scriptures call witchcraft.

AMONG BLACK PEOPLE THERE ARE MANY "JERICHO WALLS" THAT HAVE TO FALL. ONE OF THESE STRONGHOLDS IS THE WALL OF VIOLENCE.

This epidemic is certainly not limited to African-Americans, for there are studies that suggest that whites in some cases have more of a problem with illegal substance abuse. However, in the African-American community drugs can be directly related to and inherited from "Afroism." This is a vestige of African culture that survived slavery to become part of our culture in America. Drugs, spells and potions were very much a part of ancient African culture that predisposed our people to the drug culture because it was a part of religion in the motherland.

Another of Satan's strongholds that black men inherited is a "neopolygamous" legacy. This practice of having more that one woman is still accepted in much of Africa today. In early America it was perpetuated by slave masters, who used men as bucks to impregnate multiple females to produce more slave labor for the plantation.

This is the problem with getting overly influenced with Afrocentrism, unless it is sanctified by biblical and spiritual understanding. Every ideology from Africa cannot automatically be stamped good. Some ideology can become a stronghold that must be overthrown by the gospel.

Strongholds Among Black Women

Black women also have strongholds that need to be overthrown. One is "the Jezebel spirit." This is a dominating, controlling and rebellious spirit.

Jezebel, the wife of King Ahab of Israel, was a Sidonian (see 1 Kings 16:31), and therefore most likely a woman of color. "Sidonian" is the ancient term for a group of Canaanite descendants of Ham. The Greeks called them Phoenicians. Both Josephus and the African church father St. Augustine stated that Ham's people occupied Sidon. Cheikh Anta Diop, the African historian, says that Canaanite Phoenicians have a Cushite origin. The historian Pitford said that a Canaanite Phoenician priestess in Carthage had Negro features, suggesting that she belonged to an African race. Berthulon says these people had very brown skin, their lips were thick and they had high cheekbones. Historian J. A. Rogers says they were Negroes. We conclude that Jezebel was probably a black woman or, at least, a woman of color.

The Jezebel spirit can actually manifest itself through a man or woman of any race. But because Jezebel was a black woman, that spirit prefers to seek other black women to continue the legacy, which is itself a kind of witchcraft. This spirit will always seek out a weak Ahab-type of man who will abdicate responsibility and control to her. She wants someone who will let her run the show.

If African-Americans are ever going to move forward as a people, we must be committed to liberating black men. Until the men are free, the women and children cannot be free. The Jezebel stronghold resists this truth because it seeks to dominate men. It is a wall that must come down!

Codependency is another stronghold that manifests itself among black women. This bondage thinking causes many black women to become overly nurturing, taking care of everyone but themselves. Such a woman will tolerate abuse and burn herself out emotionally. This wall must come down!

The Warfare Strategy

What strategy can bring down these Jericho walls? The apostle Paul answers:

> The weapons of our warfare are not carnal but mighty in God for pulling down strongholds, casting down arguments and every high thing that exalts itself against the knowledge of God, bringing every thought into captivity to the obedience of Christ (2 Cor. 10:4,5).

To destroy Jericho, we need courageous spiritual captains like Joshua, who will lead an obedient army of soldiers, under the Commander's instructions, in the following ways:

1. Men as Prayer Warriors

God said, "March around the city, all you men of war" (Josh. 6:3). We have many women praying, but until spiritual black "men of war" are willing to get involved in spiritual warfare, we will not get the victory. We must recruit and organize our black men as prayer warriors—men with a spiritual warring demeanor who are sick and tired of what the enemy is doing to our people. They also must be men who can submit to the Joshua captains.

2. Priests Trumpeting Support

God also said, "Seven priests shall bear seven trumpets
[Hebrew *shopharim*] of rams' horns" (Josh. 6:4). In addition to
courageous captains and obedient men of war, we need some
priests who will be trumpeters. These are the ministers who
will support the warriors on the front line.

Until the ministers of our people get involved in trumpeting the truth of the message and the need for spiritual warfare, the strongholds will remain intact. At Jericho, seven
priests and seven rams' horns had to compass the city seven
times, and the soldiers could not do their thing until the
priests had finished blowing their trumpets. Seven is the number of completeness and of oaths. God is calling for black ministers to enter into covenant with other preachers in their city
to work together to completely surround the cities in America
where these strongholds exist. These ministers must simultaneously "blow the trumpets." In other words, they must
preach the Word of God to their people and to the warriors of
their congregations that the war is on and our modern
Jerichos must be taken. They must let the warriors know that
it is time to fight.

Not only do we not have enough courageous prayer captains and men of war, but also our priests have not been ready
and willing to blow the ram's horn of God's Word to signal
that it is time for war. The Bible says the priests had to make
a "long blast" at Jericho (Josh. 6:5). Ministers today also need
to make a long blast, preaching day in and day out on the warfare and its weapons, and taking the Jerichos in the black
community. The word "trumpet" in Hebrew means to lift
one's voice to utter the words and instructions of God. The
ministers must do this before the spiritual men of war can
effectively do their job.

3. A Shout in Triumph

"When you hear the sound of the trumpet," God said to Joshua, "all of the people shall shout with a great shout" (Josh. 6:5). The Hebrew *teruah*, or "shout," means to split the ears with a sound, to shout for alarm or joy, to make a joyful noise or to shout for triumph. Psalm 47:1 captures the idea: "Oh, clap your hands, all you peoples! Shout to God with the voice of triumph!"

Once the priests have spent time trumpeting the truth about warfare, the warriors around the city should shout in anticipated triumph. In our case, the warriors around the city should have a time when they can concurrently shout with the voice of triumph and joy. Can you imagine black Christians at different locations all around a city, at a specific time, simultaneously giving a praise shout of joy and triumph in anticipation of their conquest of the Jerichos that keep our people bound? What a powerful, explosive weapon!

Seven Steps in the Siege

For those using this "Jericho Siege Shout Plan," I suggest following these spiritual steps:

1. We must identify the cities and their Jerichos.

2. We must identify the courageous Joshuas.

These are praying, anointed black men who will serve as the captains over the spiritual men of war.

3. The men of war must be identified and selected from around the city.

They should come from the congregations of the priests. It would be wise to train them in spiritual warfare, and they should be men who live holy lives.

4. The priests—godly, anointed ministers and pastors who support the warriors—should be recruited and oriented.

They should agree to trumpet the Word about spiritual warfare for at least seven days (on Sunday mornings). The seventh and last message must be the "long blast," with a total emphasis on spiritual warfare from Sunday School, worship, Scripture reading, music and preaching. All the participating churches will have a similar service at the same time. After the message, the ministers, congregations and the mighty men will shout at the same time and declare a victory over that city's Jericho.

5. The warriors are to go into the areas of the city where the strongholds exist.

Just as Joshua and the warriors put the people to the sword, these warriors must put the demons to the sword of the Spirit, the Word of God (see Eph. 6:17). With this sword they walk through the neighborhood quoting God's Word, using Scriptures such as "we are more than conquerors" (Rom. 8:37) and "the one who is in you is greater than the one who is in the world" (1 John 4:4).

6. The warriors must go in and locate the "Rahab" families of black people who live in the community.

They must then witness to them, evangelize them and lead them out of bondage by praying the prayer of salvation and deliverance with them. This task will be easier and the people will be more responsive because the Jericho walls of defense will have now fallen down.

7. Once the walls are down, a fiery victory service should be held.

The last thing Joshua did was to burn the city. In our modern spiritual battles against strongholds, there should be a spiritual-

ly "fiery" service of victory where the Jericho walls of bondage
once stood. Praise God until the fire of heaven comes down to
affirm that Jericho is truly no more.

For Such a Time As This

It is my belief that God has brought us to the Kingdom for such
a time as this. He is looking for a new generation of warriors, a
new group of ebony "gibbors." To fill the ranks of the captains,
ministers and warriors, you must be ready to get involved with
the war against the forces of darkness. You who do get involved
will know the joy of the shout of triumph and the pleasing sound
of cracking and rumbling as the Jericho walls fall before you.

You will also have the satisfaction of bringing out the Rahabs
who have within their wombs the eggs of other deliverers. Rahab,
a Hamitic Amorite woman of color—a black woman—had within
her womb the eggs of deliverance. Even though she was a prostitute, she could not be fertile and activate the eggs of deliverance
as long as she was trapped inside the walls of the Jericho stronghold. Once the walls were broken down, she was brought not
only to safety but also to fruitfulness.

Joshua 6:25 says that Joshua saved Rahab and her father's
household and that she still lived in Israel at the time the
account was written. A black woman who lived all her life inside
a stronghold, who was infertile and a prostitute, now lived free
outside the walls with the people of God. She married Salmon
and became the great-grandmatriarch of David, another deliver-
er. Ultimately her crowning tribute was that this former prostitute has her name mentioned in the genealogy of our Savior (see
Matt. 1:5), in the "Faith Hall of Fame" (see Heb. 11:31) and in
the "Works Hall of Fame" (see Jas. 2:25).

Today there are Rahabs and their households waiting for the Joshuas to come, waiting for the ministers to blow the trumpets and the warriors to shout and advance. There are Rahabs waiting for the walls to fall, for their families to be brought out and for strongholds to be destroyed so that the deliverers in their wombs can be released to be agents of redemption in the end times.

Rise up ye godly men of color; rise up ye godly women of color—be courageous. There's a war going on, and victory is in our grasp. Let's break down the walls!

Chapter Five

THE FOUR HORSEMEN OF THE APOCALYPSE: IDENTIFYING RULING SPIRITS

Pastor Joseph Thompson *serves on the staff of the World Prayer Center and of New Life Church as associate pastor with Ted Haggard in Colorado Springs, Colorado.*

While I fully accept that spiritual warfare is largely similar from one race or people group to another, I also believe that subtle differences exist (because of the ancestry and heritage of the different races) and call for unique approaches to this warfare from one race to another. The opportunity to travel internationally on a fairly extensive basis has given me a fascinating perspective on spiritual warfare. I have observed that as a result of the differing spiritual climates among different countries or cultures, different ruling spirits seek to control the people. As a matter of fact, the recently discovered (at least in its present form) art of spiritual mapping lends credence to this fact.

Identifying Dark Domains

Spiritual mapping seeks to identify ruling spirits that control different areas of cities and to measure the effectiveness of targeted prayer. For example, in the city of Colorado Springs, a part of town has a proliferation of liquor stores, low-income housing and drug-related activity. Identifying and mapping these regions serves as an effective tool for intercessors who would like to pray for Colorado Springs in an organized fashion.

This system of spiritual mapping also allows churches to track and measure the effectiveness of prayers targeted at a specific area, by measuring changes in crime and drug-related statistics. Of course, it is arguable whether the decline of crime or drug use in a particular location is specifically a result of targeted prayer. If, however, churches operate from the biblical premise that indicates effectual and fervent prayer produces the power to change situations, it is not hard to accept the fact that prayer changes whole cities.

The apostle Paul further appears to confirm this when he writes that "we do not wrestle against flesh and blood, but against principalities, against powers, against the rulers of the darkness of this age, against spiritual hosts of wickedness in the heavenly places" (Eph. 6:12). Clearly, this suggests that we are indeed embroiled in a battle, and this battle is fought against spiritual forces that are hierarchical.

Numerous examples exist in Scripture of warfare occurring in the heavens between forces of good and evil, as the constant battle for the control of humanity is waged. Satan and his minions seek to establish a kingdom that opposes God and all that He represents. God seeks to reestablish the relationship that once existed between Himself and mankind through a relationship with His Son, Jesus Christ. This provides the backdrop for the warfare that is continually waged in the spirit realm.

Four Hindering Horsemen

In this context, it becomes evident that the Christian's spiritual battles are waged in the heavens against ruling spirits that directly influence the lifestyles of cities or regions. In studying the Scriptures further, I believe Revelation 6:1-8 to be a type (a foreshadowing or picture) of the spiritual forces that rule countries, territories and people groups. Here John sees the famous four horsemen of the Apocalypse on mounts that are colored white, red, black and pale. These riders no doubt represent the apocalyptic period when the Lamb of God will break the seals on the scrolls that will permit the unleashing of judgment on the earth. However, I believe they are also a present-day manifestation of spiritual forces that seek to hinder the effective communication of the gospel among the different races. We can profit by examining each of these hindering spirits in some detail.

The White Horse of Deception

John the Revelator begins by identifying the first horse of this ominous vision as a white horse upon which sits a rider who is given a crown: "And I looked, and behold, a white horse. He who sat on it had a bow; and a crown was given to him, and he went out conquering and to conquer" (Rev. 6:2).

It is not unusual for it to be assumed that this rider is Christ, since in His second coming He appears riding on a white horse (see Rev. 19:11). This interpretation, however, raises certain problems. The first is the fact that Christ, during the playing out of this scene, is in heaven opening the seals. He could not at the same time be a principal figure in the scene unraveling on earth. Second, the last three horses are clearly demonic (war, famine, death), and are released to hurt the earth and its inhabitants—a role that seems inappropriate for Christ. As the personification of good, He is incapable of evil.

The rider on the white horse actually appears to be Satan, since he has the devil's characteristic qualities. If so, his purpose for riding out on this white horse would be to conquer nations and people, bringing them under his control. This would support the fact that we wrestle against spiritual forces that dominate and control lifestyles in whole cities and regions, as previously referenced in Ephesians 6:12.

Another passage that could indicate this white horse and its rider are counterfeits of the Messiah and are on a mission to sow deceit and discord is found in 2 Thessalonians 2:3-12, where Paul says that "the man of sin" who would deceive those who do not love the truth appears in the likeness of God—which is conceivably a reference to the horse of pure white.

Such deception, according to Revelation 6:2, is the mission of the rider on the white horse. He wants to control the nations by a show of power, signs and lying wonders.

I suggest, therefore, that this rider who seeks to imitate the true King is the manifestation of the spirit of deception. He will cause many to herald his coming as the coming of the Messiah, but he will be the antithesis of good. Unfortunately, according to the preceding Scripture, there are many who will buy into the lies and deception he brings. Also, in Paul's first letter to Timothy, he says that "the Spirit expressly says that in latter times some will depart from the faith, giving heed to deceiving spirits and doctrines of demons" (1 Tim. 4:1).

False Standards of Success

This spirit of deception has already begun to do its deadly work in the African-American culture, among others. The evil and injustice of slavery created a desire in the African-American to achieve a certain standard of living in order to be accepted by the white community as more than subhuman. Part of the motivation was also to prove to himself and his white counterpart that he was just as capable of achieving success (according to the set standards that defined success). Rooted in this desire is a misguided notion of success.

The acquisition of wealth, power and control has become synonymous with success. In 1993, at a Promise Keepers event in Boulder, Colorado, Bishop Wellington Boone spoke of African-Americans on Skid Row who were offered welfare programs to rescue them from poverty. "In buying into their welfare programs they also bought into their social ideologies," he said.

This created a false standard of measuring success. As black people began to climb up the social ladder and relocate to nicer white neighborhoods, so began a mass exodus of white people from those neighborhoods. Property values dropped because of the mixing of the races. This only served to heighten the tension and bad blood between blacks and whites, and many blacks became not just ethnically *conscious* but ethnically *controlled* as a means of self-preservation.

One of the "strongmen" associated with deception is racism. This spirit is rooted in fear and misunderstanding. Unless the Church presents a united front to the world on this issue, we are unlikely to witness a true movement of God in our nation. A concerted effort must be made to desegregate our churches. We must allow the Spirit of God to fulfill Jesus' prayer in John 17:11 that we (the Church) are one, just as He and the Father are one.

The Plight of the Family

Another natural consequence of this quest for success is the breakdown of the family. As men sought to become wealthy by any means, many of them turned to drug dealing, which was thought to provide a handsome and quick financial return. Others turned to armed robbery and other such fraudulent practices, also hoping to reap a large return. Inevitably, many of them ended up in prison, leaving their young families dependent on the generosity of the welfare system and their sons to grow up disillusioned with life and the hope of a decent standard of living.

Because of the vacuum created by the absence of a father, it becomes difficult for the young African-American in these circumstances to develop a concept of God as a loving and caring Father. He carries with him a distorted image of the role of a father. In his quest to emancipate himself from a lifestyle that holds no hope, he turns to the streets and its attendant evils, such as drugs, indiscriminate sex and violence. Gang membership offers him a temporary sense of security and a false sense of family. In reality, this keeps him from growing and from seeking a more fulfilling lifestyle.

As violence and sex become the outlets for pent-up aggression, such persons inexorably become anesthetized to evil. Low self-esteem sets in, especially for the young African-American female who equates love with a sexual interest in her body. This then leads to children giving birth to children, who are dependent on the welfare system for their livelihood. It becomes an increasingly entangled web from which there appears to be no escape.

The spirit of deception seeks to convince the young African-American that the way out of this lifestyle is not through discipline, hard work or an education. It suggests that the rapid amassing of material wealth provided through an alternate lifestyle of drugs, turf wars, violence and the use of sex as a business will provide an escape. Ironically, this is a lifestyle choice that guarantees violent death or destruction.

Clearly, this white horse that rides out with so much evil intent must be confronted with great spiritual understanding. We must thwart its efforts to deceive and ultimately destroy African-Americans' trust in, and dependence on, the lordship of Jesus Christ.

The Scriptures teach us in Proverbs 13:12 that hope deferred makes the heart sick. We must restore hope among the people in our communities through the reordering of our value systems. While we should not be opposed to the acquisition of material wealth, we must show that when it becomes an end in itself, motivated by selfish desire, it is destructive—"The love of money is a root of all kinds of evil" (1 Tim. 6:10). Ask Tupac Shakur. Ask O. J. Simpson. "There is a way that seems right to a man, but its end is the way of death" (Prov. 14:12).

We must refocus our attention on the realities of Kingdom living. Jesus Christ is Lord, regardless of the circumstance. In order to live victorious and fulfilled lives, we must place our trust in His unchanging Word in the midst of an everchanging world.

The Red Horse of War

The second horse in John's vision is a red horse, which symbolizes war and wanton destruction: "Another horse, fiery red, went out. And it was granted to the one who sat on it to take peace from the earth, and that people should kill one another; and there was given to him a great sword" (Rev. 6:4). This horse and its rider are commissioned to take peace from the earth and wreak havoc among the nations. This is a picture of war and strife.

The fallouts of war are innumerable. Fear motivates people to do the unthinkable. In war, fear becomes a dominant spiritual force. People are uncertain of their safety. Consequently, they degenerate to subhuman levels, fighting for their very survival. At such times, looting and even killing are not uncommon, as people will do anything just to get food, water or a place of shelter. These circumstances tend to create dehumanizing conditions, which further serve as a distraction from daily living and the successful completion of set tasks and goals.

There is a spiritual context in which this becomes applicable to the African-American. War is symbolic of strife and disunity, and the Bible states that "where envy and self-seeking ['strife,' KJV] exist, confusion and every evil thing are there" (Jas. 3:16). Also, "If a house is divided against itself, that house cannot stand" (Mark 3:25). Strife, disorder and disunity are manifest in numerous ways from one social group or society to another. This produces effects similar to the conditions created by war, including the lack of social and moral order.

In our African-American communities, the devil has enabled broken marriages, alcoholic/abusive parents, loose morality, low self-esteem, sibling rivalry, and AIDS and other STDs, among numerous other destructive behavioral patterns. These conditions force the young African-American to turn to avenues that he or she believes will provide solace and comfort. The inevitable consequence is drug abuse, multiple sexual partners, gang banging and other expressions of violence and abuse. These behaviors in turn lead to high mortality rates and an absence of peace and stability among this demographic group.

The situation must be identified for what it is: a spirit of war that ultimately seeks to destroy and kill. It is only when this spirit is identified that we are able to destroy it and break its stronghold over our communities. The manifestations of this spirit, which are so rampant in our communities, are not just a socioeconomic problem that can be successfully addressed by the welfare system. It is fairly evident that none of the numerous social programs has even made a dent in this growing spiritual problem.

However, we are seeing inroads in communities where the Church is recognizing the spiritual root of this problem and addressing it with spiritual warfare, as well as an open display of God's love. The absolutely incredible programs run by Tommy Barnett and Jim Bakker in Phoenix and Los Angeles are examples of the transformation that can occur in the inner cities where the drug culture is so prevalent.

LACK OF APPRECIATION FOR LIVING CREATES A DEARTH OF ANY KIND OF VALUE SYSTEM THAT WILL PRODUCE A FRUITFUL LIFE.

It is therefore of vital importance to the proper evolution of our culture that we address spiritual problems with spiritual solutions. Intercession, spiritual warfare, the breaking of generational curses, deliverance and proper reeducation (through the Scriptures) of our communities are essential if this spiritual stronghold is to be destroyed.

The sense in which the drug culture, the absence of fathers in the homes, alcoholism and various other social ills relate to war and strife is evidenced by the fact that all of these detract from focusing on living purposeful lives. This lack of appreciation for living produces a lack of desire to invest in anything of lasting value and, consequently, creates a dearth of any kind of value system that will produce a fruitful life.

The Black Horse of Famine

The third horse is a black horse, representing famine:

> When He opened the third seal, I heard the third living creature say, "Come and see." So I looked, and behold, a black horse, and he who sat on it had a pair of scales in his hand. And I heard a voice in the midst of the four living creatures saying, "A quart of wheat for a denarius, and three quarts of barley for a denarius; and do not harm the oil and the wine" (Rev. 6: 5,6).

Distorted Focus Destabilizes

As a natural consequence of war, the spirit of famine seeks to destroy the very fabric of society by creating inhumane conditions of living. As stated earlier, when our focus is on conflict, famine is frequently the consequence. People are too busy warring to find time to concentrate on planting and harvesting the food that is necessary for their very survival.

There are a couple of ways in which famine as a driving spiritual force becomes a hindrance to the ability of the African-American to receive the gospel. The living conditions and environment in the ghettos and in poorer, predominantly black neighborhoods do not provide adequate hygiene or healthy eating habits. This is primarily because of the lack of resources to provide decent infrastructure to support these communities.

Interwoven with this spirit of famine is a spirit of poverty. Famine has manifest itself as poverty in the poorer black communities where people have learned to survive on whatever is available because they don't have the means to provide themselves a healthier diet. They also lack the proper education to afford them the opportunity to provide a better standard of living. Consequently, they often become resigned to what they consider to be an inescapable plight.

All this can lead to alcoholism and drug addiction as a means of escaping the harsh realities of the environment. When this mind-set takes root in certain communities, people become insular, and life loses its value. This subtle scheme of Satan is designed to keep African-Americans conditioned to believing that they have been abandoned and forsaken by a God who claims to be love personified. If their poverty-ridden and malnourished lives are evidence of a loving God, then they may ask whether they are not better off without Him.

This satanic web of lies has been woven so deeply into the fabric of present-day African-American culture that many communities believe the only recourse they have to ensure their continued survival is to pursue any means available (good or bad) that provides some semblance of respite from their hardship, no matter how temporary the respite.

This is not an unlikely strategy of Satan, since his ploy is to keep people bound in such abject poverty as to cause them to become morally bankrupt. The connection here is the fact that one who is morally bankrupt is ill equipped to recognize that the battle for survival is as much a spiritual battle as it is an economic one.

Those who do not see the real enemy they are fighting are often unable to articulate a proper strategy to defeat the foe. Under these circumstances, the Word of God holds little value in waging an effective campaign against Satan. The focus on physical survival distracts many from the more relevant task of spir-

THE RELENTLESS STRUGGLE FOR PHYSICAL SURVIVAL IS ONE OF THE MORE SUBTLE SCHEMES OF SATAN TO KEEP THE YOUNG AFRICAN-AMERICAN FROM ACTIVE PURSUIT OF GOD.

itual survival, which itself produces insight for physical survival. This is not unlike the picture painted earlier of war as a catalyst to famine. Just as war distracts from the business of everyday living, so the relentless struggle for physical survival distracts from the more necessary pursuit of spiritual survival. This is one of the more subtle schemes of Satan to keep the young, struggling African-American from the active pursuit of God.

The Bible paints a clear picture for us in this regard:

Therefore do not worry, saying, "What shall we eat?" or "What shall we drink?" or "What shall we wear?" For after all these things the Gentiles seek. For your heavenly Father knows that you need all these things. But seek first the kingdom of God and His righteousness, and all these things shall be added to you (Matt. 6:31-33).

The primary focus of this passage is not the fact that people are seeking after material provision but rather the fact that seeking after a relationship with God is the avenue to providing a godly lifestyle attended by the necessary material blessings.

Victim Mentality and Mistrust

The second way in which famine becomes a hindrance to the African-American's ability to receive the gospel lies in the fact that these impoverished communities begin to take on a sense of victimization. They see themselves as the unfair victims of the lowest socioeconomic class of a society that is somewhat intolerant of the less fortunate. This in turn causes these communities to become distrusting of the existing civil authority structure and interdependent on themselves. They believe that no one outside their own communities is interested in their advancement.

The situation also breeds fear, from the lack of exposure to any other form of community living beyond that in which they have been raised. People tend to fear what they do not understand. From the African-American's perspective, the system is designed to work against them to keep them from ever succeeding. This accounts for many African-Americans' distrust of the police and other such civil authorities.

The issues become larger than just poverty and take on a whole new dimension that includes racial tension. The white man becomes the reason for the black man's poverty and, by the same token, becomes the enemy. How then can blacks accept the "God of the white man," who, seemingly, has dealt so harshly with African-Americans? Little wonder that the trend these days is for the African-American to identify with his African heritage and to follow the religions of his ancestors.

Unfortunately, many traditional African religions are inherently animistic and lead away from the one true God. The Old

Testament prophet Amos states his case as follows:

> "Behold, the days are coming," says the Lord GOD, "That
> I will send a famine on the land, not a famine of bread,
> nor a thirst for water, but of hearing the words of the
> LORD. They shall wander from sea to sea, and from
> north to east; they shall run to and fro, seeking the word
> of the LORD, but shall not find it. In that day the fair vir-
> gins and strong young men shall faint from thirst"
> (Amos 8:11-13).

If Amos were alive today, witnessing the problems of this
generation, he would probably see a clear picture of these verses
in a large number of our communities. Psalm 48:2 states that
God resides in "Mount Zion on the sides of the North"—but
many people in our society are running to the East and to New
Age religions to seek after the Word of the Lord. Obviously they
will not find it there, just as the African-American will not find
the solution to his problems in African religions. This famine is
spiritual and can only be relieved by establishing a meaningful
relationship with the Lord Jesus Christ.

The Pale Horse of Death

The ultimate purpose of Satan, according to John 10:10, is to
steal, to kill and to destroy. He will stop at nothing to ensure
that this process is carried out consistently and succinctly. Thus,
the fourth and final horse in John's vivid vision is a pale (mangy)
horse of death.

> So I looked, and behold, a pale horse. And the name of
> him who sat on it was Death, and Hades [hell] followed

with him. And power was given to them over a fourth of the earth, to kill with sword, with hunger, with death, and by the beasts of the earth (Rev. 6:8).

If there has been any doubt as to the truly demonic origin of these horsemen, it is certainly laid to rest in this verse. The passage makes abundantly clear what evil intentions this horse and rider have. Death, the Bible says, is the final foe that shall be defeated (see 1 Cor. 15:26). The scene here is a last-ditch effort by Satan to rally his troops for a final foray against the kingdom of God. The Bible is explicitly clear about the fact that this effort is an exercise in futility. Satan and his demonic hordes are soundly defeated, resulting in the appropriate epitaph, "O Death, where is your sting? O Hades [hell], where is your victory?" (1 Cor. 15:55).

This truth must penetrate the hearts and minds of our African-American communities. The ploy of Satan here is to convince our African-American brothers and sisters that their economic, social and spiritual plight is beyond salvage. Nothing is further from the truth. The reason Jesus died on the cross for the sins of mankind was, and still is, the redemption of mankind from every plight that has befallen us and, by so doing, to reconcile us with our Creator.

This rider on the pale horse works hand in hand with deception, war (strife) and famine to ensure that the African-American views his situation as helpless and hopeless. If this spirit successfully takes hold of our communities, both physical and spiritual death will be the consequence of that stronghold. We must pray fervently, interceding on behalf of our African-American communities (particularly for the younger generation) that they will turn their focus to Jesus Christ and His completed work at Calvary.

These demonic strongholds, represented by the four horse-men, must be utterly destroyed to enable African-Americans to break free from the mind-sets of racial inequality, lack of identi-ty, poverty and numerous other destructive social patterns. It is, however, only after the enemy has been properly identified that the proper weapons can be employed to defeat that enemy. We are committed to the battle, knowing that the victory is already assured.

It is my sincere and fervent prayer that this revelation of the spiritual strongholds we are up against will enable us to fight the battle more precisely and effectively. We must remember always that:

The weapons of our warfare are not carnal but mighty in God for pulling down strongholds, casting down arguments and every high thing that exalts itself against the knowledge of God, bringing every thought into captivity to the obedience of Christ, and being ready to punish all disobedience when your obedience is fulfilled (2 Cor. 10:4-6).

Chapter Six

A FATHER'S COMMITMENT TO OVERCOME PERSONAL STRONGHOLDS

Rev. Edgar D. Barron *is vice president of field ministries for Promise Keepers and an associate minister at Riverside Baptist Church in Denver, Colorado.*

Ever hear the term "boys of summer"? That's what baseball players are called. What young boy hasn't dreamed, every now and then, of stepping up to the plate with the count full, the bases loaded and his team down by one run?

In that regard, I was as normal as any other red-blooded American boy. I loved baseball, and I was pretty good at it. As clearly as though it were yesterday, I can remember riding my bike across town to get to practice. I'd slip my glove over the gooseneck handlebars of my gold Schwinn Stingray and race as fast as I could through the bustling streets of the small town where I grew up.

As I look back, the ballpark wasn't really all that far. But to me, an eight-year-old future Hall-of-Famer, it seemed like several country miles. Besides, I couldn't wait to get there. I can still recall the smell of the freshly mowed grass, the sound of the other kids splashing in the nearby public pool, the excitement of running toward the coach as he emptied the balls and bats onto the ground.

Where Was Dad?

With all those fond memories, this was obviously a special time. It would be several years later before I realized this time held other memories as well—memories that are not as innocent as those of a Little Leaguer with big dreams.

I really liked my coach, Mr. Satterfield. He was one of the most kindhearted men I've ever met. He really brought out the best in me. He made me feel special, and I wanted to do my very best for him. I guess that's a trademark of a good coach, mentor and leader—the ability to bring out the best in others.

It felt good—no, it felt great—when Mr. Satterfield acknowledged me. It was as though he was in some way relieving my pain. You know, like holding your hand under cold running water after you've burned it on the stove. As long as you hold it under the water, the pain subsides; but as soon as you remove it, the pain returns with greater intensity.

Why was I in pain? What void was Mr. Satterfield tapping into? The void in my life stemmed from the absence of my father.

Don't misunderstand. My dad was still with us. It would be another four years before he and my mother divorced. He was physically present, but I needed more than his presence. What I needed was *him*. I needed to be validated by my dad. What was missing was having my dad join in with what was important to me. I wanted to share my dreams with him. I wanted to hear him instruct me and encourage me.

As my own son was growing up, I wondered, *Will I be a better dad to him than my own father was to me? Or will I end up hurting my son in all the ways my father hurt me? What can I do to break the chain of bad father-son relationships?*

It's not that my dad was evil. In fact, I looked up him. I wanted to grow up to be just like him—brave, strong, never letting his emotions show. But I was the antithesis of him.

I had fears—lots of them—and I couldn't seem to keep my emotions in check. I felt weak compared to him, and I was sure he knew it.

I can't remember my dad telling me that he loved me, but I can remember his lighting up when he told of my accomplishments to a friend or business associate. It felt great to hear my dad—my hero—brag about me.

So I began a pattern of performing for acceptance. I thought that maybe if I became "the best" at everything, Dad would play catch with me in the backyard, or show up for my basketball games, or take time off work for a school event. But he never did—not even once.

So I tried harder. And it worked, sort of. Hearing Dad's praise wasn't the same as hearing the words "I love you," but it felt good, and it was better than nothing. I also learned that performing also worked with others, like my coaches, scoutmasters and teachers. All I had to do was continue to perform well and all would be well.

Covering Failure with Deceit

Then I learned about the downside of the performance game—failure. If I failed to perform, I would fail to be accepted. Since failure is a part of life, I had to find ways to deal with it . . . and I did. Deceit became a major part of my life. I figured that if I could convince those around me that I was perfect, then they would accept me.

I also decided to avoid any activity that had a high risk of failing. I was living a very controlled and structured life—and I was only 11 years old.

Then one day when I was 12, my dad said, "Your mom and I are getting a divorce, and we want to know who you want to stay with."

Besides feeling shock, since I had no idea their marriage was in trouble, I remember having absolutely no desire to live with my father. "I'll stay with Mom," I said. "She'll need a man around the house." I showed no emotion and didn't ask any questions. I just turned and went upstairs to bed.

My dad moved out a few days later. Now, more than ever, I had to perform well. But despite attempts to manage everything around me, things in my life were falling apart. My entire being yearned for my dad's love and affection.

Then I discovered something to fill the void. Something that gave me physical and emotional comfort—pornography. When I was in pain, looking at pornography made me feel good, at least for a few minutes.

When I was 19, I left home for college. My pattern of performance was paying dividends. However, I soon realized how ill equipped I was for this new stage of life. The risk of academic and social failure was great. I was losing control. I needed to do something to fill the emptiness I was feeling, so I added drugs to my pornography obsession. I rapidly became addicted to both.

My fear of failing caused me to drop out of school even though I was on the dean's list. The guilt and shame of my addictions drove me into deeper levels of hiding and deceit. I didn't have any close friends because I was afraid they might

THE GUILT AND SHAME OF MY ADDICTIONS DROVE ME INTO DEEPER LEVELS OF HIDING AND DECEIT. BUT I STILL KNEW HOW TO PERFORM.

find out who I really was. But I still knew how to perform. I landed a job with a large aerospace company and immediately moved into management. On the outside, I appeared to have it all; on the inside, I was dying.

New Relationship, New Faith

Then I met Lucia. She was beautiful, charming and, most importantly, she loved Jesus. Because of her, I came to know Him, too. With my newfound faith, I knew I would have to give up my addictions. I kicked the drug habit, but I couldn't shake the pornography problem.

Lucia and I started to date, and soon we became engaged. I figured that once I got married I wouldn't need pornography anymore. But it had a death grip on me. I couldn't understand it. My love for Lucia was deep and true. For the first time in my life I was starting to feel complete.

Then I had the scariest thought of my life: *What if Lucia found out who I really was?* I chose to continue to hide from her.

For years I fought the battle alone. I thought that if I could just do enough for God, He would take this sin away from me. But performing for God didn't work.

Then, at a men's retreat, I surrendered. God was telling me I had to confess my addiction to pornography to my wife. It was the hardest thing I've ever done. It is only by the grace of God that our marriage survived. Throughout months of Christ-centered counseling, I began to see the root causes of my behavior. Although I take full responsibility for everything I did, I was able to understand the severe impact of not having received my father's unconditional love. And I vowed not to make the same mistake with my children.

As I learned to exchange my pattern of performance for God's unconditional love, I was able to love those around me. I can honestly say that I have never missed a single one of my son's sports events. I even coached his baseball team. Because of Coach Satterfield, I knew the impact I could have on the other boys as well.

Periodically, I break away from my busy schedule to go to school events with my daughters, too. I want them to know that what they do is important to me. And my wife and I are communicating on a level deeper than I could have imagined possible!

God had one more wonderful surprise for me. When my dad was diagnosed with cancer, he suddenly discovered what was most important in his life. He reconfirmed his commitment to the Lord and sought to spend more time with his children. As a result, our relationship blossomed.

At the end, as I sat with him at his bedside, I put my arm around him and told him I loved him. He turned to me, looked into my eyes and softly said, "I love you, too, son."

The stronghold was broken.

Chapter Seven

BUILDING A PRAYING CHURCH

Dr. Jerome McNeil, Jr., *is pastor of Christian Chapel CME Temple of Faith Church in Dallas, Texas, and director of the Dallas affiliate of the Congress of National Black Churches.*

In a society filled with racism, sexism and classism, many consider themselves outcast citizens. Living in a culture that devalues them, these persons need the Word of God. When the need to be affirmed is so overwhelming, among people of color in particular, the importance of the house of God is amplified. Isaiah 56:7 is an invitation from God for all such outcasts to come to His holy mountain:

Even them will I bring to my holy mountain, and make them joyful in my house of prayer: their burnt offerings and their sacrifices shall be accepted upon mine altar; for mine house shall be called an house of prayer for all people (*KJV*).

This reference targets those who were shunned by others but whom God welcomed into the intimacy of prayer in His Temple. It is with this confidence that ordained men and women of God prepare His House for all people and make it what it was called to be—a house of prayer.

Jesus' Passion for Prayer

Jesus recalled Isaiah's prophetic statement when He saw that God's people had forgotten His purpose to make the Temple a gathering place for outcasts (see Matt. 21:13; Mark 11:17; Luke 19:46). Although His directive infuriated the religious leaders and teachers of the Law, Jesus affirmed that we are to take seriously the role of God's house as a house of prayer.

Jesus Himself always undergirded His words and ongoing ministry with prayer. He was saturated in the concepts of a life devoted to prayer. He recognized, instructed and demonstrated prayer in every level of his life.

During their brief tenure as Jesus' disciples, His followers could have asked Him to share with them His method for accomplishing any number of works. They could have inquired of Him His technique of healing by touch or at a distance. They could have sought the answers to the mysteries of the universe or the secrets of riches and eternal life. They could have asked His divine insight on the composition of persons—what makes man *man*. Jesus might have shared with them previously unanswered questions of death, demonic possession and evil in the universe.

Instead, in Luke 11:1, Jesus' disciples inquired and sought out the Master with the burning request, "Teach us to pray." Obviously, the disciples realized that prayer was the power behind the Master and His ministry. And without hesitation, Jesus taught them the prayer that has become for many the "Model Prayer," or what is commonly called the Lord's Prayer.

Pastors Committed to Prayer

Now, would it not seem logical to consider that if Jesus saw such significance in prayer, that those of us who are called to lead the Church He instituted would also reflect His passion for prayer? If prayer is so important to the heart of God and to our existence, how can we transform our churches into houses of prayer?

To move in this direction, we must individually become genuinely committed to a life of prayer. A hunger and thirst for communion with God must be in operation in our lives. We must begin to experience prayer at new levels and seek to become intimate with Jesus on a daily basis. Our lives and ministries must become totally dependent on the power of Jesus through prayer.

After we are convinced of God's promises to bless us through prayer and after we have entered into a practice of constant prayer, this new lifestyle will become infectious in many ways.

You can begin to refresh your knowledge of prayer and its importance from your own Bible; then move to the many books dealing with prayer. The works of E. M. Bounds contain detailed and explanatory analyses of prayer. Andrew Murray's books are also an excellent resource.

Ask God to open your heart for prayer. Ask Him to create a hunger and desire to know more of Him in every aspect of your life. Begin to journal your prayer requests and answers. Maintain a regular devotional time of Bible study and prayer. Begin to saturate your life with prayer thoughts. Put the power of prayer into operation in all daily occurrences. Observe how your focus on prayer will begin to alter your conversations, your decisions and the results of your ministry.

WHEN PRAYER HAS BECOME THE AIR WE BREATHE AS LEADERS—AS PASTORS—LET US THEN APPROACH THE ISSUE OF MAKING OUR MANY "TEMPLES" INTO HOUSES OF PRAYER.

Recount for others the scriptural references to the effects of prayer in the situations you encounter. Deposit prayer nuggets wherever you go. Use prayer as a means of encouraging others during your usual day-to-day contacts with them. When people sense that you take prayer seriously, they will recognize a new power in your life.

Building a House of Prayer

When prayer has become the air we breathe as leaders, let us, as pastors, then approach the issue of making our many "temples" into houses of prayer. We can meet God at any place with the right attitude of heart.

Early in their history, God's people heard from Him from the mountaintop. Later, the Temple became a special place of prayer and communion with Him. Our own houses, our personal temples, must be in focus as we approach God's holy mountain. When any place has been designated a sacred gathering place for all people, we must identify it as a house of prayer.

In the primary sense, of course, God's people are His "house" (see Acts 2:47, *KJV*; 1 Tim. 3:15). But the local church that wants to become a house of prayer for its community should maintain the awareness that God brings His presence in a special way to the house where His people assemble. The place where all the disinherited, disenchanted, disillusioned, disgruntled, dismayed, disgusted, defeated and denied may come is to God's house of prayer. God invites people to come and will provide deliverance, comfort, hope and joy to those who assemble to seek Him.

Consecrating the Sanctuary

To prepare your house for the hurting, begin by praying around the grounds of the property, asking God to touch all who cross onto the holy ground. Inside the house, enter and anoint each doorway, praying that God would move upon the hearts of whoever enters this house of prayer. Pray over each pew along the walls and every place where someone will be seated or standing.

Cover the house by saturating it initially with the prayers of some chosen prayer warriors who believe that God's ways are mysterious. This prayer covering is a process of allowing the presence of God to permeate the entire place of worship. The warriors should pray together with a level of expectancy in their spirits and then begin walking in silence and praying over specific needs and desires for the church.

They should pray over the offering baskets or collection plates, that God will pour out His blessings and bring forth fruitful tithes and offerings. They should pray over the pews and, with God's discerning power, at spots where specific people sit. Pray for peace, healing and deliverance. This should become a regular focus of the prayer warriors of your congregation.

With these preparations, the assurance of God's indwelling power will become evident in many ways. A sense of the presence of the Lord will manifest itself, and a change in the atmosphere will become noticeable when one enters the temple. The transforming power of the Lord will cause some supernatural things to happen. Foremost is that people will feel His presence. As indicated in Isaiah 56:7, once God brings us into His holy mountain, He will make us joyful in His house of prayer. Because the house of prayer has been saturated to the full extent, the awesome anointing of God will come forth.

Communicating the Vision

For your church to become devoted to prayer, you must communicate a vision for breakthrough to your congregation. You can create an unusual expectancy that things will happen beyond a visible means of perception as you incorporate this emphasis into your sermons and messages. Here are some suggested topics:

A Praying Church Recognizes God's Promise
A Praying Church Recognizes God's Purpose
A Praying Church Recognizes God's Power
A Praying Church Recognizes God's Provision
A Praying Church Recognizes God's Presence

A Praying Church Recognizes God's Position
A Praying Church Recognizes God's Preeminence
A Praying Church Recognizes God's Passion
A Praying Church Recognizes God's Package (Faith,
   Hope, Love)

Remind the congregation that when we pray without ceasing, we are opening opportunities for God's favor, focus, finances and fulfillment to come into existence.

Prayer Warriors

The enthusiasm and expectancy of people, young and old alike, will rise up in praying churches. All churches, it is hoped, will have some level of focus on prayer; but a church devoted to a bold prayer commitment must pray seven days a week, 365 days a year. Every church will encourage all members to pray, but a church focused on capturing Jesus' passion for prayer will call forth certain people to place special emphasis on prayer. These people will be the congregation's prayer warriors.

The pathway to transforming a meeting place into a house of prayer must include a course of systematic training steps on prayer. It is important to train leaders and prayer warriors/intercessors in the various aspects of prayer.

To do that, you can sponsor a series of prayer clinics or seminars at your local church. In this clinic or seminar, expose the participants to the different aspects of prayer. Give sample written prayers for special situations and allow time for focused prayers to be uttered in accordance with these directives. Additionally, a practical approach to prayer and its purpose and promise may be taught, preached and demonstrated regularly in the local church.

A vital prayer life and inner healing must be operational in the lives of our prayer warriors in order to see change and balance in the spiritual climate of our churches. We cannot change others or ourselves with only good intentions or with ability or will power. We must deepen our roots of depending on God's nurture. We can only sow the seeds of power through our prayers.

Special Prayer Times

You may want to schedule an opportunity for the entire church to participate in 24-hour prayer vigils. Bulletin inserts on prayer directives and prayer needs, along with sample intercessory prayers, are helpful. Topical Bible studies on prayer, along with question-and-answer periods, are a good educational tool.

Pastors must teach the people that we rise to new heights as we lower ourselves into the deep confines of our prayer closet and then ascend to the heights of God's visibility.

To demonstrate your own growing commitment to prayer as a priority and to recruit a core group of prayer warriors, schedule a prayer vigil, or a "It's Prayer Time!" meeting, monthly or bimonthly. The prayer vigil will bring forth individuals with a sincere commitment to prayer. It will develop warriors who do not pray to be seen but who have an earnest desire to weep, groan and yield before the throne of God.

These meetings must be guided by the Spirit but should also take into consideration that the vigil is not to be undertaken without a focus. Include a brief study time and opportunities for open prayer. A portion of time may be devoted to the anointing of the sanctuary, doors, pews, pulpit, altar, fellowship hall and choir loft. The unified surrender of maintaining an atmosphere of God's presence will make these vigils a powerful venture. The magnetic power of God's presence will invade the house, and the evidence of signs and miracles will without a doubt come forth to sanction this direction in prayer.

Remember that the numbers present at these vigils are always under God's divine counting system, whether there be 3 or 30. God's effectiveness is matched by His anointing power and presence.

Ideally, the preparation of the atmosphere in the sanctuary where the prayer vigil is conducted will add to the benefits of the prayer experience. Lowered lighting, meditative music and comfortable clothing enhance the worshipers' receptivity. Allow individuals freedom to pray silently or aloud, sitting in the pews, standing up, kneeling at the altar and even lying prone before the Lord. The focus is to go to Jesus with thanksgiving, adoration, confession, supplication, intercession and requests for forgiveness.

Sunday Morning Prayer

In the course of establishing your church as a house of prayer, utilize every opportunity to expose the people of God to your prayer focus. The morning worship experience should always offer a time of intimacy and prayer, both individually and corporately. Beyond the traditional opening invocation, prayer times at the altar can prove to be a very powerful vehicle for confession and both spiritual and physical healing.

Offer times for prayer concerts and prayer encounters through the worship experience by grouping two to three persons together as prayer partners. Have the prayer partners pray for personal needs and against generational curses. Ask them to include prayers of adoration, confession, intercession, thanksgiving for family blessings, and petitions for the forgiveness of sins.

Allow the pairs or triads of prayer partners to develop throughout the service for intercessory prayer. They may offer corporate intercession or words of knowledge to be shared in an intimate setting. These times of prayer may also be interspersed with selected hymns or songs with special significance for prayer. Assure the congregation of the power of these prayers, as affirmed by the Lord's promise in Matthew 18:20: "For where two or three come together in my name, there am I with them" (*NIV*).

Incorporating intense prayer into your morning worship service will mobilize a greater power base to accomplish the many visions you and your members have for the church's ministry. We can make all the difference in our lives and the life of the church through a radical approach to prayer.

Prayer Rooms

To keep the house of prayer before the minds of the people, designate a room specifically for prayer. This intimate setting should be simple and appropriate for private prayer times. It may be utilized for 24-hour prayer-a-thons or daily prayer times. Literature in the form of pamphlets, tracts and Bibles will be helpful in the room. A pillow for kneeling and a journal for prayer requests and answers could offer added emphasis.

Corporate Warfare Prayer

The opportunity for free expressions of prayer throughout a service can mobilize a church to warfare potential. A church that places unlimited attention on prayer will face much opposition from the forces of evil but gain unceasing power from on high.

When a church embraces this concept of prayer, God has unlimited access to the body of believers. This is because God has ordained that a praying church results in the reformation of believers.

OFTEN PEOPLE PRAY THAT GOD WILL SEND REVIVAL WHEN, IN FACT, PRAYER SHOULD BE MADE FOR THE REFORMATION OF THE CHURCH.

Often people pray that God will send revival when, in fact, prayer should be made for the reformation of the Church. When something is reformed, it is improved, reshaped and changed—or else it is removed! If God took a picture of today's Church, it would reveal a Church so out of form that it needs to be re-formed. If there is no reformation, there is no revival.

A church can best be reformed in prayer by committing to praying as a body in the assembly. Such audible prayers carry tremendous weight against the forces of evil. When a congregation begins to pray out loud in one accord, the heavens take notice. Sometimes people are hesitant and hindered by audible or corporate praying. However, the unlimited power that goes forth from these prayers is without measure and beyond comprehension. Calling upon the Lord forcefully and unashamedly in the house of God accesses His power to penetrate His mysteries as we *pray what we can't see, and believe what we can't know.*

The Lord is depending upon us to allow Him to have full control of our lives. The yielded saint is a dangerous warrior in the battle of good and evil. God knows our potential when we use the weapon of prayer in all things. Develop a direct access to God through this power in prayer. And remember:

Praying people prevail.
Praying people are prepared.
Praying people are powerful.
Praying people are principled.
Praying people are persistent.
A praying people perform.

May you grow strong as you establish your house of prayer. Increased prayer in the house of God means victory in life and power in the streets, in homes, offices, jobs, family, finances, schools and every place where Christians fight the good fight.

Keep on praying!

Chapter Eight

PERFECTING PASSIONATE PROCLAMATION THROUGH PRAYER

Dr. Carison Adams *is senior pastor of St. Paul Missionary Baptist Church and founder of GAP Prayer Ministries in Marion, Indiana.*

How often I have stood in my pulpit to preach the Word of God but failed to spend quality time in prayer with God! I hate to admit it, but I have many times represented the voice of God without having stood before the very presence of God.

How often have we as pastors stood before a group of people who were depending upon us to guide them through the Scriptures for better understanding of God's truth, without first asking for His guidance ourselves? How much of our preaching and teaching is actually exercised out of the energy and futility of our own flesh?

Many times in our preparation for the biblical message, we eagerly walk into the sacred text, searching for what to say; and when we come out with a message, we presumptuously go directly into the speaking event. We justify our presumption because of the quality time spent in the Word of God. We read and overhear what the characters are saying. We probe and question, make notations and get impressions. We come out of the text in the presence of the congregation and say that there is a word from the Lord.

THE SECRET OF GOOD PREACHING IS TO PREPARE THE MESSAGE FROM THE KNEELING POSITION.

However, our messages should be more than techniques and outlines. In addition to (or in spite of) what we have learned in our hermeneutics and homiletics classes, the pastor's true preparation has to begin with becoming a changed person. That change can only come from time spent with God in prayer.

The Secret to Great Preaching

The secret of good preaching is to prepare the message from the kneeling position. The transformation that occurs in the lives of believers comes from lying on their faces before a holy God. In this humble position of prayer, our great God can get hold of us. He begins to reveal to us who we are so that we may become more like Him. The prophet Isaiah had this experience:

In the year that King Uzziah died, I saw the Lord seated on a throne, high and exalted, and the train of his robe filled the temple. "Woe to me!" I cried. "I am ruined! For I am a man of unclean lips, and I live among a people of unclean lips, and my eyes have seen the King, the LORD Almighty" (Isa. 6:1,5, *NIV*).

Just as Isaiah's realization of his own ruined state became apparent in front of the Master of the universe, we too must approach His throne in a state of humility. With heads bowed low and with hands uplifted, we must be purged in the presence of God by coals of fire touched to our minds, bodies and souls before we can hear the words emanating from the throne. God's getting hold of us alters the messengers so that the message we share can be life-changing for our people.

Can you imagine what impact our preaching would have if the voice of the Lord were truly represented through the time we spent in prayer and preparation? Our greatest deficiency is not in education, resources or ideas, but in *prayer*. Yet, how many preachers select their text and titles without asking counsel of God? How many topics have been assigned to you in answer to prayer?

The Pastor's Prayer Life

It is assumed that preachers, teachers and church staff members have an above-average prayer life. Yet an article in *Leadership* journal said that "by our own admission, a national survey revealed the average American pastor spends less than 10 minutes a day in prayer."[1]

According to that same study, the highest pastoral frustration is the gap between the prayer life that pastors know they need and their inability to make that happen. How can we preach the eternal Word of God and pray fewer than 10 minutes a day?

Preachers and teachers can learn methods to prepare technically proficient messages filled with truth and practical daily application. However, we cannot preach or teach with power unless we spend time with God. The power of God adds fire to knowledge. We must understand that authentic biblical expository study must be the result of authentic biblical praying. When we spend time in prayer, the people who hear us will know it—just as they will know when we do not spend time in prayer.

It is difficult to spend time in prayer. There is so little time, and we spend it reading the biblical text, studying commentaries and doing word studies because it is important to teach the people sound doctrine. We also have many other duties—people to call on, administrative tasks to do, meetings to attend.

So what is the answer to the obviously hectic life of those who are in ministry? How do we deal with the frustration of knowing that prayer is necessary, but we lack the ability to improve our prayer lives? When ministers are dealing with the daily tasks and activities that scream for their time, the deadline for that sermon is still approaching. While we are spending all of our time doing "holy work," we come to the realization that this work has begun to dull our awareness of our need to be alone with God. Intellectuality, rather than spirituality, begins to characterize our preaching and teaching ministries.

Years ago I became aware of the poverty of my own spirit. I was aware of the depletion of my power. In fact, I almost had pulpit burnout because I did not cultivate my prayer life. I realized that my moments with God were hurried moments and I was hurting the heart of God, His people and myself. This awareness brought about a restoration in my prayer life as I turned to the life of Jesus and began to imitate His prayer habits.

Jesus, the Model Preacher

The prayer life of Jesus is our ultimate model of developing a prayerful life that will impact our preaching. Jesus had tremendous pressures and expectations as multitudes followed Him daily. Yet the Bible tells us that He took time to communicate with the Father: "Very early in the morning, while it was still dark, Jesus got up, left the house and went off to a solitary place, where he prayed" (Mark 1:35, NIV).

The time Jesus spent in prayer brought power to His ministry. We wonder why there are no miracles happening in our ministries. We speculate as to why people are not receiving healing from emotional and physical illnesses in our churches. We question why marriages are being destroyed and people are not being delivered from addictions. We wonder why people do not understand and always support our vision. The answers to these questions are to be found in our prayerless lives. We need to have the disciplined prayer life that Jesus had in order for us to have His power.

Jesus plainly promised, "Verily, verily, I say unto you, He that believeth on me, the works that I do shall he do also; and greater works than these shall he do; because I go unto my Father" (John 14:12, KJV). If we indeed want to do the greater works, we will need the greater prayer power.

In the Sermon on the Mount, Jesus admonishes us to pray, and promises us blessings: "But when you pray, go into your room, close the door and pray to your Father, who is unseen. Then your Father, who sees what is done in secret, will reward you" (Matt. 6:6, NIV).

Private Places, Public Power

The Bible shows us examples of people who were mightily used by God. Most often, from Moses to David to Paul, we find that those people had a powerful communication with the Father. In fact, Scripture will bear out that all those who were ever mightily used by God had a prayer closet.

Abraham had his altar. "From the Negev he went from place to place until he came to Bethel, to the place between Bethel and Ai where his tent had been earlier and where he had first built an altar. There Abram called on the name of the LORD" (Gen. 13:3,4, *NIV*).

Daniel had his chamber:

> Now when Daniel learned that the decree had been published, he went home to his upstairs room where the windows opened toward Jerusalem. Three times a day he got down on his knees and prayed, giving thanks to his God, just as he had done before (Dan. 6:10, *NIV*).

Peter went up on a rooftop: "About noon the following day as they were on their journey and approaching the city, Peter went up on the roof to pray" (Acts 10:9, *NIV*).

Habakkuk went to a prayer tower: "I will stand at my watch and station myself on the ramparts; I will look to see what he will say to me, and what answer I am to give to this complaint" (Hab. 2:1, *NIV*).

Where is your prayer closet?

Prayers for the Preaching

One way to begin to transform our preaching comes through the people in our ministries. A preservice prayer by such people will have a tremendous impact on the preaching and teaching of their ministers.

On Sundays, before I step out to deliver the Word of God, I am literally bathed in prayer as select men from the church gather around me to intercede on my behalf. Oh, the power and strength that then enable me to speak the oracles of the Divine One!

On the day of Pentecost, Peter preached a powerful message and 3,000 souls received salvation (see Acts 2:41). Peter had the prayer covering of the church in order to preach with the anointing of God (see 1:14). Furthermore, in the upper room, 120 disciples of Christ had prayed for 10 days. It was after all this prayer that God transformed Peter for service.

Do you remember the spiritual condition that Peter found himself in during the last days Jesus walked the earth? He was weakened by fear (see John 18:25-27) and paralyzed by his lack of self-confidence that God could use him for ministry (see John 21:15-17). Peter, who became known as "Rock," had previously reflected the strength of a pebble. So when he became transformed, he knew it was the presence of the Holy Spirit and the power of a prayerful life that had changed his life forever.

When was the last time we preached and 3,000 souls were saved?

Note
1. *Leadership* (Winter 1982), n.p.

Chapter Nine

THE PRAYER THAT HEALS ABUSE

Pastor Donn Charles Thomas *is senior pastor of Victory Assembly of God in Stone Mountain, Georgia, and a renowned songwriter and worship leader.*

In a healthy, functional family, parents take a position of authority. This healthy authority allows parents to affirm their children's personhood by wisely giving appropriate consequences for wrong behavior, providing constructive teaching and encouraging right behavior.

But parents are human beings. In the process of trying to meet the needs of their children, they make mistakes. When parents use their authority to force children into performance, when they apply harsh standards of judgment or use their position of parental authority to satisfy their own needs and desires for importance, power or emotional or even sexual gratification, abuse occurs.

Family is the child's place of safety; it should not be a place of fear. When a child's trust is violated emotionally, verbally, physically or sexually by a parent or adult, destructive forces are released within the child. These forces may only be healed by Christ Himself and His healing community.

After a time of wounded relationships between the Corinthian church and Paul, the apostle could eventually refer to the healing of that wound (see 2 Cor. 2:5-8).

My Experience with Abuse

I grew up with six older sisters and a twin brother in a city in northwestern Ohio. My mother was, and is, a deeply committed Christian woman in her local Church of God in Christ. She raised us up to fear and respect God (see Prov. 1:7; 22:6) and nurtured us and loved us with every bit of energy she had—and she had plenty. We sang gospel songs and prayed together.

My mother prayed openly, and constantly revealed her faith. I vividly recall her praying for us to have food in the house because my father had taken the money from his job and spent it on alcohol. I remember my mother praying and fasting for several days for the opportunity to purchase the house we were renting. On the last day of her fast, while she was standing on the front porch, the owner drove up and gave my dear mother the deed to the house. On the spot, my mother worshiped and praised God "like a joyful mother" (Ps. 113:9) for hearing her prayers and granting her a home. We all praise God for her.

My family's problems of abuse started with the alcoholism of my father. Whenever people were around, he was full of mirth and humor. He loved telling jokes and having people laugh. But there was a darker side to Dad. He would often curse at Mom and us children. He would become physically abusive and fight my mother. We children saw this and were terrified, but we tried to protect our mother by fighting back. Many times the police would come and take my father to jail. The abuse went on for many years.

EVEN THOUGH I WAS A COMMITTED CHRISTIAN, I DEVELOPED A "SPIRITUALITY" THAT PERMITTED DENIAL, AND I BURIED MY PAIN AND ANGER FOR MANY YEARS.

Even though I was a committed Christian, such early experiences caused deep pain and anger. As a defense mechanism, I developed a "spirituality" that permitted denial, and I buried my pain and anger for many years.

However, my pain and anger were real. I remember wanting my father to hold and hug me. Apparently, that was too difficult for him. Once, when I was six or seven years old and my parents were separated, my father took me and hid me from my mother so that he could force a reconciliation. The police were called in and I was classified as a missing child.

On another occasion, when I was getting ready to go to university, my father gave me a dollar and laughed in my face. I became so enraged that throughout the 30-minute ride to school, I was unable to talk to my friends. It was the grace of God that helped me through that quarter of school, both financially and emotionally. In those days, I only acknowledged that Mr. Thomas birthed me; he was my biological father, nothing else. If anyone had asked if Mr. Thomas were my father, I would have given him a polite, matter-of-fact yes, without elaboration.

I wanted to be loved by my father, but I received little or nothing in return. I began looking for a father in other men, particularly my pastor. God used my pastor to heal some of my pain and anger.

After university, I married my longtime friend. We developed a deep and abiding love and appreciation for one another. She had a beautiful, healthy relationship with both of her parents. Eleven years into our marriage, her father died. We were both devastated. This incident inspired thoughts of my own father. I began to think, *What would I do if my father died today?* After the funeral services, I was tormented both by thoughts of my father's abuse and of his dying.

One day my wife and I were talking about having a family. She was disturbed by the emotional distance between my father and me. She wanted this to be healed so that when we had our family, our children wouldn't experience my pain and anger. Then she made a most piercing statement that rendered me emotionally naked: "You hate your father!" No one had ever said this to me before. I had developed a spirituality that protected me from having to disclose my anger and confront my father.

This spirituality also made it next to impossible to be healed from my pain and anger. I had no place to hide. I had no defense against this raw, powerful truth coming from my wife. God used her to confront me with a sin that had debilitated me. I could no longer prevent the disclosure of my hatred. Eventually, after first trying to protect myself by denying what was obvious to her, I surrendered both to the Lord and to my wife; I went to the quietness of my office and fell on my knees, weeping and praying.

The Prayer That Heals Abuse

The Lord began to speak to my heart and said, "How can you love Me whom you've never seen and hate your brother whom you see every day? You are a liar (see 1 John 4:20). This verse also applies to your father."

I begged the Lord to forgive me for hating my father. I told Him that I didn't have the ability to forgive after being so full of pain and anger for so long. The Lord told me that He would provide me with the grace to forgive my father.

Then I had a major surprise. The Lord told me to get up and call my father and ask him to forgive me for my hatred toward him. I said, "No, Lord, why don't You tell him to ask forgiveness for what he took our family through, particularly me?"

Then the Lord spoke to my heart again, saying, "I accepted you with all your sin and forgave you for all your offenses against Me and declared you righteous. Now you accept your father and ask him to forgive you for hating him."

I rose from my knees and sat in my desk chair. I picked up the phone and dialed. "Dad," I said, "how are you? How's the weather? What's Mom doing?" Usually, when we talked, it was for two to three minutes at most; then I would ask to speak to Mom. But this time, I had to obey the Lord.

I blurted out, "Dad, would you please forgive me? I have hated you for many years." I began to weep. "You hurt me when you fought with and abused Mom; you accused me of very ugly things that I didn't do. You hurt and shamed our family for so many years. Your laughing at me while you were drunk and your giving me a dollar for four years of university were very painful. My friends laughed at you."

I said everything that I needed to say. Then I heard my father's faint crying over the telephone. I had never seen or heard him cry before. In the midst of his crying, he asked me to forgive him for all the things he had done to me.

After I hung up the phone, I sat quietly in contemplative prayer and meditation. Then the healing broke through. It was as if Jesus Himself had begun to put His hand inside me and pull out the bitterness, pain, anger and hatred.

I didn't feel total freedom at that moment, but I knew that a great force of healing had occurred in me in depths that I would experience for days, months and even years. As a matter of fact, this deep healing is still going on.

Dad has changed very little—but I have been changed for life because I confronted my sin of hatred. Also, my family began to change its attitude toward Dad because of how I began to love and respect him.

Steps Toward Healing

How do African-American males, and for that matter females and people of other races, get healed from the devastation of family abuse?

First, *acknowledge that the abuse happened.* Without this honesty, healing can never be experienced. Second, if possible, *confront the person* who is the cause of your pain and anger. The victim and the victimized are bound up together—it could be that the Lord will heal you both. Third, know that *we must always go to God in prayer* about everything, including abuse, hatred, pain and anger.

We can hear God say:

Come here to me all of you who are working hard and carrying too much, and I will refresh you. Here, take my yoke upon you and learn from me, because I am gentle

and simple at heart, and you will experience refreshing
deep down in your lives. You see, my yoke is easy and my
burden is light (Matt. 11:28,30).[1]

Note

1. Frederick Dale Bruner, trans., *The Christbook: A Historical/Theological Commentary: Matthew 1-12* (Waco, Tex.: Word Books, 1987), p. 437.

Chapter Ten

LIVING BEYOND YOUR HURTS

Evangelist Georgia Ellis *is a seminar and conference speaker affiliated with the True Way Evangelistic Church of God in Christ in Dallas, Texas. She is also president and founder of Deliverance Outreach Ministry.*

It was a time of crisis in my life. I struggled through many days and nights in turmoil and hurt. There was also deep frustration in my spirit because of what was going on in my life at that time. After all, I was a born-again believer, a spirit-filled Christian and a faithful church attendee.

I was also a faithful wife and mother, and I loved working with people day after day, praying and counseling with them. We helped people come to a place of peace in their lives. We would preach and teach God's Word as we prayed for others.

Yet I was broken on the inside.

One morning, while I was lying in bed, the Spirit of God impressed upon my heart to review several key Scriptures. Doing so helped me come to a place of peace during my hours of hurting and frustration. I had discovered that prayerful communion with God has the power to restore us to live beyond our hurts.

God reminded me that as long as the earth remains, we will have crises and problems in our lives. If there were no sickness, we would never know that God heals (see Ps. 107:20). If there were no storms, we would never know that God speaks peace (see Mark 4:39). If there were no hurting people, we would never know that He binds up the wounds of the brokenhearted (see Isa. 61:1).

I am confident that, like me, as you read daily nuggets from

IF THERE WERE NO SICKNESS, WE WOULD NEVER KNOW THAT GOD COULD HEAL; IF THERE WERE NO STORMS, WE WOULD NEVER KNOW THAT GOD WILL SPEAK PEACE; IF THERE WERE NO HURTING PEOPLE, WE WOULD NEVER KNOW THAT HE BINDS UP THE WOUNDS OF THE BROKENHEARTED.

God's Word and share your struggles with Him in prayer, He will bring you to that place where you will be encouraged to know that staying in His presence brings fullness of joy (see Ps. 16:11).

What Is God Doing in Our Lives?

The silent times in our lives are times when we must find a quiet place in God, a place where the enemy cannot find us, a place where we can discern His plan.

God loves us and desires to heal our brokenness. He has a wonderful and victorious plan for our lives. When we see nothing of Him, when we hear nothing from Him, when it seems as though God is nowhere to be found, we must realize that whatever is going on, He has all things in control. This is not a runaway world; nothing happens that God has not allowed. God often uses times of struggle to "promote" us further into Him from our distress, or to take us to another level of anointing.

To overcome your trials, allow your mind to think God's kind of thoughts and to realize that nothing is impossible with Him! Do not accept that the mountain you currently face is impossible for God to move. Remember that He is a miracle-working God committed to bringing you out of your distress. The impossible is made possible with the help of a sovereign God.

So when it seems as though nothing is happening in your life, use that time to say no to the enemy of the mind and yes to the will of God. For it is God's will that we prosper and be in good health even as our soul prospers (see 3 John 2). When fear has been conquered in our lives, we are surely on our way to a higher level in God and to a place where we can receive His promises.

So what is God doing? He's taking you to your place of destiny. Don't allow anyone or anything to stop you from getting there.

God Will Remove the Reproach

Often the enemy comes to discourage us through our tests and our hurts. It appears, when we are in the test, that God has forgotten us or that He will not fulfill His Word. Philippians 4:19 lets us know that He will supply all our needs according to His riches in glory, because of what Christ Jesus has done for us.

Elizabeth was barren—she had no children—yet she and her husband Zacharias were godly people. Zacharias was a priest, and the Bible says in Luke 1:6 (*NIV*) that "both of them were upright in the sight of God, observing all the Lord's commandments and regulations blamelessly." Although they loved God with all their hearts, Elizabeth was barren.

Yet Deuteronomy 7:9 says that if we are obedient, the Lord our God is faithful to keep His promise for a thousand generations and that He will constantly love them who love Him and obey His commandments. Through our obedience, He will bless us and make us into a great nation. He will make us fertile and give fertility to our grounds and to our animals so that we will be blessed above all nations (see Deut. 7:14).

Zacharias and Elizabeth knew the Word of God and its promises. They had served God from their youth, they had grown ripened with age, yet they had no children. But God is so faithful to His word that no matter how long you may have waited for your breakthrough, God is watching over His word to see that it is performed (see Jer. 29:10). If you will seek Him with all your heart, you will find Him.

Zacharias and Elizabeth had this kind of trust, and finally they found favor with the Lord. They became the parents of John the Baptist; this is what prompted Elizabeth to affirm that "the Lord has done this for me, . . . In these days He has shown his favor and taken away my disgrace among the people" (Luke 1:25, *NIV*).

Don't allow the devil to tell you that you'll never come out of barrenness in your ministry, in your finances, in your health and in your life. For you *will* come forth as Elizabeth did.

When you think on the things happening in your life, you may ask yourself, *When will my marriage be whole? When will my ministry come alive and be productive? When will my finances change?* Remember that help is on the way right now. God is removing the reproach, and He is turning your life around.

He Wants to Take You by the Hand

We read in Mark 5:41, "He took the child by the hand, and said to her, 'Talitha, cumi,' which is translated, "Little girl, I say to you, arise.'"

Jesus wants us to be whole. He wants us to arise out of our hurts, out of our sickness, out of our depressions, out of our situations of discomfort. He wants us to seek life in the Word of God. It will give us food for the soul that causes us to have strength to go through anything in our lives.

When Jesus said to the little girl "Talitha, cumi," which meant in Aramaic, "Little girl, I say to you, arise," she immediately got up and walked (see Mark 5:42). Then Jesus commanded that she be fed to strengthen her physically.

Jesus is also lifting us out of our beds of circumstances, and we must eat the Word of God that we may be able to stand with strength.

The account says that before Jesus reached out His hand to lift the little girl out of the bed, He put everybody out of the room (see v. 40). For us to come out of our pitiful situations, we must allow Jesus to put everything negative out of our minds. Jesus wants to lift us to a place of absolutely knowing that we do not have to remain in a state of helplessness. We must have a state of mind that says *I will arise and receive what God has for me.*

Living Beyond the Hurts

As born-again believers, we sometimes feel that because we are Spirit filled, we are not supposed to have to go through difficult situations or problems. And if we do, then we're not supposed to talk about them or seek any counseling.

Scripture records that "when the Lord saw that Leah was unloved, He opened her womb" (Gen. 29:31). Suppose Leah had not shared her testimony with us. We wouldn't have known that she was a woman whose unhappiness became a blessing to humanity. Her testimony shows us that we can find God in every area of our lives, and we can live beyond our hurts. Her experience should encourage us because it gives us insight into how God looks at a person. The Bible says that Leah had "weak eyes" (Gen. 29:17, *NIV*). God doesn't look at us for our outward beauty but for our hearts. God dealt with Leah's situation as He saw it. Knowing our own hearts, God's love for us will bring us through anything we may face in life to a place of joy, no matter how unbearable our circumstance might seem.

Leah's great faith in God kept her going from day to day. Although the Bible never states that she won Jacob's love, she became the mother of six of his 12 sons, who would go on to become leaders of the 12 tribes of Israel. Furthermore, Leah's hurt and sorrow produced a greater understanding of Jacob's God, and it enriched her confidence in Him.

Rachel, who was loved by Jacob, was attractive and beautiful to look upon; but she was disappointing to God on the inside. She was a selfish and jealous person. The Bible never mentions anything about her love for Jacob or for Jacob's God. She chose to govern her own life, seeking after the pagan gods of her father, Laban. She was even a thief, stealing the gods from her father's house.

Leah experienced the pain of living with a husband who did not love her. She learned to take her pain and her need to God. But Rachel's attitude left little room for gratitude to God. Even though she knew she was loved by Jacob and that she was beautiful to look upon, she was bitter.

We must remember the importance of prayer and reliance upon God as we face whatever obstacles come our way. Prayer enables us to use those obstacles as stepping-stones on which to climb up to the next level toward the presence of God.

Chapter Eleven

REBUILDING OUR CITIES
THROUGH PRAYER

Dr. Walter Fletcher, Jr., *serves as pastor of prayer development and adult Christian education at Hillcrest Church in Dallas, Texas.*

When God wants to manifest His great handiwork in the earth, He does not send an angel. He works through mankind— through His people who are available to listen in prayer and obey His instructions—and especially through the leaders of His people. The Lord declared through the prophet Ezekiel, "So I sought for a man among them who would make a wall, and stand in the gap before Me on behalf of the land, that I should not destroy it" (Ezek. 22:30).

Nehemiah, who was appointed governor in charge in rebuilding the city of Jerusalem after the captivity, was such a man. As a matter of fact, his achievement of transforming a city that had been literally destroyed by its enemies is so instructive that God gave us a book named after Nehemiah. Not only is the book instructive, but the method by which Nehemiah turned failure and defeat into restoration and recovery is also significant for those who are interested in helping to rebuild the morally and socially crumbling cities of today.

That method is prayer.

In the book of Nehemiah, prayer is mentioned more than 13 times in connection with the rebuilding of Jerusalem. With the repeated examples of the praying of Nehemiah and the people, we are to understand that if our cities (or nations!) are to be recaptured from the devastation, waste and destructive force of the enemy, *we must pray.*

The City's Source of Comfort

Nehemiah's name means "consolation of Jah," or comfort of Jehovah. He is a picture for us of the One who has come to equip us and guide us into the complete restoration and rebuilding not only of the communities where we live but of our personal lives as well. Nehemiah's work would ultimately culminate in the sending of the Holy Spirit, that divine Comforter sent by the Father, through the Son, Jesus Christ, to bring us the comfort and assurance that all things are possible with God (see John 14:16-18).

Before we can rebuild our cities we must have the constant leadership and direction of the Holy Spirit. If we attempt to rebuild without Him, we are doomed to frustration and failure. The psalmist reminds us that "Unless the LORD builds the house, they labor in vain who build it; unless the LORD guards the city, the watchman stays awake in vain" (Ps. 127:1).

A Proper Diagnosis

Before a doctor can cure any form of sickness or disease, he must first properly diagnose the cause of the illness. Nehemiah had to be made aware of the true condition of the city of Jerusalem and his people in order to be sensitized to their need. He tells us it happened in this way:

> It came to pass in the month of Chislev, in the twentieth year, as I was in Shushan the citadel, that Hanani one of my brethren came with men from Judah; and I asked them concerning the Jews who had escaped, who had survived the captivity, and concerning Jerusalem. And they said to me, "The survivors who are left from the captivity in the province are there in great distress and reproach. The wall of Jerusalem is also broken down, and its gates are burned with fire" (Neh. 1:1-3).

A proper understanding of the true condition of the city must include the fact that *its walls of protection are broken down.* People are at risk of being destroyed by forces that only prayer can conquer. So our cities cry out for prayer as a primary tool in the task of rebuilding.

Nehemiah was in a place of great advantage. He was not a lowly captive as his brothers had been. He had risen to the position of cupbearer to King Artaxerxes of Persia, where the Jews had been taken into captivity. He was very comfortable and well insulated from the struggles his brothers were experiencing back in Jerusalem. As a matter of fact, he was not even acquainted with their condition until he asked about them.

What he discovered was that although his kinsmen had escaped death, they were barely living. And although they had survived their captivity, they were still bound by their circumstances. They had no walls to protect them; all were broken down. And to make matters worse, the gates had been burned with fire.

Does this not, in some way, describe the devastation that has taken place in our cities that lie ravaged by the destructive forces of Satan? And does it not even pertain to the people of God, spiritually speaking? Due to our own sin and failure to obey the Lord, we have been held captive by the spirit of this age, now working in the sons of disobedience (see Eph. 2:2). And although we are alive physically, we are not experiencing the fullness of His life.

Because we citizens of the modern city have turned from God's laws, we have no walls of protection about us. Because we have refused to make God our defense, we are left vulnerable to slums and slumlords, drug-infested neighborhoods, prostitution, broken marriages, broken homes, broken lives. Truly our walls are broken down and our gates are burned with fire.

What can we do? Nehemiah shows us the way back to restoration, recovery and security in God. It happens through getting and maintaining a focus on prayer.

The City and the Prayer of Contrition

We have the first focus in prayer at the very beginning of Nehemiah's work in rebuilding the city. It is a prayer of contrition and confession:

So it was, when I heard these words, that I sat down and wept, and mourned for many days; I was fasting and praying before the God of heaven. And I said: "I pray,

LORD God of heaven, O great and awesome God, You who keep Your covenant and mercy with those who love You and observe Your commandments, please let Your ear be attentive and Your eyes open, that You may hear the prayer of Your servant which I pray before You now, day and night, for the children of Israel Your servants, and confess the sins of the children of Israel which we have sinned against You. Both my father's house and I have sinned" (Neh. 1:4-6).

Nehemiah comes before God in prayer with a broken and contrite heart. The word "contrition" means a sense or feeling of deep sorrow and grief for having offended a holy and benevolent God. The word is also associated with true penitence and the sincere resolution to live in obedience to God.

God's people need to pray prayers of contrition for the city, and prayers that those who occupy the cities will also be led to repentance.

The Lord promises certain benefits to those with truly contrite hearts. For one thing, God draws near: "The LORD is near to those who have a broken heart, and saves such as have a contrite spirit" (Ps. 34:18). And Jesus promises, "Blessed are those who mourn, for they shall be comforted" (Matt. 5:4). In fact, salvation can only come after contrition: "For godly sorrow produces repentance leading to salvation" (2 Cor. 7:10).

Even in the midst of the deepest decay of our cities, where there are those whose hearts have been truly broken and contrite over their sin and offenses against God, He draws near. It is only unconfessed sin that keeps God at a distance. God loves us so much that He waits at the door for the returning prodigals of our cities. He is full of mercy and loving-kindness to the brokenhearted.

The difficulty is that many in the city are so far from having a contrite and penitent spirit! There is often an attitude of false pride behind our attachment to the city. As grand as are the skyscrapers and housing developments we build, they also provide the crowds and the walls in which sinful practices hide. For too many, the city represents an attitude of independence and even rebellion against God. Christian sociologist Jacques Ellul wrote:

> The city . . . is both the place where man's conquest is affirmed and the memorial to that conquest. . . . It is because the city is such a place that man's triumphant march without God can take place . . . she is a tower in order to seize for herself what belonged to God, she is a wall to protect herself against God's interventions, she is stone blocks to fold within her bosom that conquest.[1]

In our cities we see many who seek comfort in the midst of difficulties due to sin and failure, but they miss the key ingredient: *mourning* over sin and failure. The comfort of God is reserved for all who mourn.

Believers in the ancient city of Corinth provide a case in point. Just as sexual sin is a part of the moral decay in our cities, so it was a problem even in the church in Corinth. The apostle Paul rebuked it in no uncertain terms. At first the Corinthians had defended it in pride, refusing to mourn the sin (see 1 Cor. 5:1,2). Eventually, however, God's Word pricked their hearts and their consciences, and Paul was later to write:

> For observe this very thing, that you sorrowed in a godly manner: What diligence it produced in you, what clearing of yourselves, what indignation, what fear, what vehement desire, what zeal, what vindication! In all

things you proved yourselves to be clear in this matter.
. Therefore, although I wrote to you, I did not do it for the
sake of him who had done the wrong, nor for the sake of
him who suffered wrong, but that our care for you in the
sight of God might appear to you. Therefore we have
been comforted in your comfort (2 Cor. 7:11-13).

**GOD'S PEOPLE MUST PRAY FOR THE CITY, THAT HE
WILL BRING US TO OUR KNEES IN CONTRITION
FOR THE SINS WE THINK TO HIDE IN ITS DENSITY.
ONLY THEN CAN THE CITY BE HEALED.**

Comfort for the city can come only after contrition. This is
why God's people must pray for the city, that He will bring us to
our knees in contrition for the sins we think to hide in its density. Only then can the city be healed.

The Prayer of Petition

Nehemiah continued in his praying, moving into a time of
petition:

O Lord, I pray, please let Your ear be attentive to the
prayer of Your servant, and to the prayer of Your servants who desire to fear Your name; and let Your servant
prosper this day, I pray, and grant him mercy (Neh. 1:11).

A petition is a request, usually a solemn or formal supplication for something urgently needed or desired. Nehemiah's
solemn petition was that the Lord God would "prosper" him

and "grant him mercy" in his activities on behalf of the city of Jerusalem. Can you imagine anything more appropriate than God's people today lifting up prayers for success—not for our private programs and projects, but for the well-being of our communities?

Nehemiah knew that anything he would attempt without the divine assistance of God wouldn't get very far. Further, his petition was rooted in the character of God Himself—in His mercy. There is the recognition here that healing the city does not depend at all on human endeavor but on the gracious empowering of God's Spirit to accomplish His design.

God's mercy is grace extended in the midst of personal failure and defeat—attitudes that grip large sections of our greatest cities. Yet God has designed His mercy for just such situations: to be given to the undeserving and the sinful.

The prophet Jonah came to understand this truth after some difficulty. Like Nehemiah, Jonah was sent to work on behalf of a city, the city of Nineveh. Here was a community filled with paganism and idolatry. At first, Jonah did not understand that God's grace was to be petitioned for just such sinfulness. So Jonah tried to flee from his responsibility as a godly leader. It was in the belly of that great fish that he perceived the truth that the people of Nineveh were actually candidates for the mercy of God (see Jon. 2:2-8).

In the midst of this terrible experience, Jonah sent up a petition to God. He realized not only that the Ninevites were rebelling against God's grace but also that Jonah himself was forsaking God's mercy.

Do God's leaders realize that the very mercy God extended to them in calling them to positions of ministry and leadership is the same mercy He wants to extend to the modern "pagan" city? If so, during these times of such tremendous spiritual and social needs in our land, we will lift up prayers of petition for the cities instead of abandoning them.

Continuing "Instant" in Prayer

Many of God's people have prayed for years over their cities, only to see very little change. It is important that we recognize fully the firm grip that moral, spiritual, economic and social diseases have on the city. Like the evil spirit the disciples could not cast out of the man, "this kind does not go out except by fasting and prayer" (Matt. 17:21). The demonic spirits are trying to wait us out, hoping that we will become discouraged when we do not see immediate results to our prayers. It is for just such situations that the apostle Paul counseled us to be "continuing instant in prayer" (Rom. 12:12, *KJV*).

The old King James phrase "instant in prayer" means praying so urgently that you do it anytime, anywhere—even constantly. In Nehemiah's case, his concern for the city of Jerusalem was so urgent and he had wrestled with the concern so much that his entire appearance was affected:

> And it came to pass in the month of Nisan, in the twentieth year of King Artaxerxes, when wine was before him, that I took the wine and gave it to the king. Now I had never been sad in his presence before. Therefore the king said to me, "Why is your face sad, since you are not sick? This is nothing but sorrow of heart." So I became dreadfully afraid, and said to the king, "May the king live forever! Why should my face not be sad, when the city, the place of my fathers' tombs, lies waste, and its gates are burned with fire?" Then the king said to me, "What do you request?" So I prayed to the God of heaven (Neh 2:1-4).

Nehemiah had not only prayed constantly for Jerusalem and petitioned the king; he prayed urgently at King Artaxerxes' question, asking the God of heaven to help him in his petition to the king. And sure enough, he found in the course of being faithful to what was put into his hands—in continuing *instant* in prayer—that God was at work to answer his prayer.

Do we feel urgently and earnestly enough about the plight of our cities to wrestle with God and ourselves and the demonic spirits on their behalf? Whether or not there are immediate, visible results to our prayers, when we have prayed we must believe that God not only hears prayer but that He also answers prayer. Scripture tells us that the eyes of the Lord are over the righteous and His ears are attentive to their prayer (see Ps. 34:15). Even if there seems to be a delay, be assured that the answer is on the way.

In other words, faith must be mixed with our prayers for the city. We must realize that God sometimes delays the answer in order to develop faith. He is not merely a rewarder of those who seek Him, "He is a rewarder of those who *diligently* seek Him" (Heb. 11:6, emphasis added). The apostle Paul put it this way: "Praying always with all prayer and supplication in the Spirit, being watchful to this end with all perseverance and supplication for all the saints" (Eph. 6:18). By virtue of the blood of Jesus Christ, the heavens have been opened to us. So God invites us as He did Jeremiah, "Call to Me, and I will answer you, and show you great and mighty things, which you do not know" (Jer. 33:3).

Prayer Walking for the City

God answered the prayer of Nehemiah. He was released by the king on a short-term basis to look into the welfare of his people in the city of Jerusalem. When he arrived there, he did something very significant. He arose in the night and went about prayerfully surveying the condition of the wall and the gates of the city. No doubt he found some parts of the city undisturbed by the war, but he also saw the sordid sights and the walls and gates that had been destroyed by fire. He returned, saying,

> "You see the distress that we are in, how Jerusalem lies waste, and its gates are burned with fire. Come and let us build the wall of Jerusalem, that we may no longer be a reproach." And I told them of the hand of my God which had been good upon me, and also of the king's words that he had spoken to me. So they said, "Let us rise up and build." Then they set their hands to do this good work (Neh. 2:17,18).

Here is a wonderful example of principles we can apply in order to "prayer walk" our communities. First, note that Nehemiah went about simply observing the condition of the city and its walls without giving anyone the slightest indication of what God had in mind. When walking your neighborhood or community, you are not trying to draw attention to the fact that you are pulling down the strongholds. Rather, as you walk your area, in a true spirit of prayer you ask God to let you see your neighborhood through His eyes.

Nehemiah saw both the bad and the good in his survey, just as you, no doubt, will see both aspects of the state of your community. Nehemiah saw places like the Valley Gate, the Refuge Gate, the Serpent's Well and the burned walls that must have been eyesores. We could liken them to the slums and other places in our neighborhoods that also give rise to spiritual sores. They represent the satanic oppression, uncleanness and immorality that are poisoning the lives of the families in our communities.

Nehemiah also saw some good things as he moved on—positive aspects of the city such as the Fountain Gate and the King's Pool. These speak of the points of blessing and refreshing in our communities. While we want to identify and pray over those areas that do not reflect God's ideal, at the same time we must not fail to thank God for those things (jobs, businesses, churches, schools, etc.) that promote the welfare of our communities and neighborhoods.

We need to pray for the decision makers of our city—those who are directly or indirectly involved in the state of the community. As a Christian leader, do you pray regularly for the mayor and city council and other officials of your city? We have a scriptural mandate to pray in this way. Paul wrote to Timothy:

> Therefore I exhort first of all that supplications, prayers, intercessions, and giving of thanks be made for all men, for kings and all who are in authority, that we may lead a quiet and peaceable life in all godliness and reverence. For this is good and acceptable in the sight of God our Savior, who desires all men to be saved and to come to the knowledge of the truth (1 Tim. 2:1-4).

We have often overlooked this injunction to pray for all men, especially those who are the policymakers and have direct influence on our social outlook and the character of our cities. But, of course, the goal is that the gospel of the kingdom of God might have a reception in the community among the lost, that we who are to be light and salt might allow it to do its work (see Matt. 5:13-16).

Alert in Prayer

The people were inspired by the Spirit of God through Nehemiah's sharing the vision to see their city rebuilt. They put their hands to the work with great enthusiasm. But it wasn't long before the ene-mies of God's people arose to oppose the restoration process (see Neh. 4). What did Nehemiah do? He returned to what had brought them through to this point: *prayer*.

Specifically, the people took a united stand, staying alert in prayer against the enemy.

> Now it happened, when Sanballat, Tobiah, the Arabs, the Ammonites, and the Ashdodites heard that the walls of Jerusalem were being restored and the gaps were beginning to be closed, that they became very angry, and all of them conspired together to come and attack Jerusalem and create confusion. Nevertheless we made our prayer to our God, and because of them we set a watch against them day and night (Neh. 4:7-9).

Using the strategy of a unified effort in prayer, Nehemiah set up a watch against the enemy. He and the people did not just sit on their laurels after praying. As we must do, they maintained a constant prayer vigil against the real enemies of the city, the real forces that had caused its decay.

The psalmist knew the reality of being alert in prayer:

> As for me, I will call upon God, and the LORD shall save me. Evening and morning and at noon I will pray, and cry aloud, and He shall hear my voice. He has redeemed my soul in peace from the battle that was against me, for there were many against me (Ps. 55:16-18).

The Lord Jesus told His disciples to be alert in prayer: "Watch and pray, lest you enter into temptation. The spirit indeed is willing, but the flesh is weak" (Matt. 26:41).

Peter wrote to warn the believers of the danger of not being alert against the enemy: "Be sober, be vigilant; because your adversary the devil walks about like a roaring lion, seeking whom he may devour" (1 Pet. 5:8).

When Christian leaders call God's people to come together in a unified prayer effort against those forces that have sought to destroy the city and to pull God's people apart so that the work of the Lord will not be accomplished, the works of darkness are overthrown. You see, the tactic of the enemy is to intimidate by inciting confusion. What one man or group or church cannot do alone, God's people as a united and alert prayer front can accomplish.

Strengthened in Prayer

The enemy does not quit easily. Although Nehemiah's opponents did not achieve success in their attempt to divide and conquer the people of Jerusalem, they proceeded to their next tactic: fear, through accusations and threats. The enemy accused Nehemiah of rebuilding the walls in view of a rebellion in which he would set himself up as king, and threatened to report this to the king of Persia. "They all were trying to make us afraid," Nehemiah wrote, "saying, 'Their hands will be weakened in the work, and it will not be done.' Now therefore, O God, strengthen my hands" (Neh. 6:9).

Nehemiah recognized this strategy of accusations and threats as an attempt to weaken the people's hands in the work of rebuilding the city. The enemy wanted to discourage them, hoping to create a mood of fear. But Nehemiah continued to work because he knew He served an almighty God who had given him this task.

This is one of the benefits that Christian leaders have over secular attempts to save the city. When mere social policies fail, there is no spirit higher than the human spirit to rely on. But Christians retain faith and pray for the strength needed to continue in the face of failure, false accusations and threats.

The work of the Lord is not for the fainthearted. The Scriptures tell us that if we faint in time of adversity, then our strength is small. But thank God, we do not stand in our own strength to do His will. Paul reminds us, "For God has not given us a spirit of fear, but of power and of love and of a sound mind" (2 Tim. 1:7).

Again, the psalmist wrote regarding the enemy and God's ability to deliver: "Cast your burden on the LORD, and He shall sustain you; he shall never permit the righteous to be moved" (Ps. 55:22).

The Prayer of Thanksgiving

Nehemiah realized the fulfillment of the dream of seeing his city rebuilt and the gates of authority and security in place. What had not been achieved in years, as the city had lain in ruin, was accomplished in record time. What more should be done than that prayers of thanksgiving should be offered unto God for His divine assistance in this great work of rebuilding the city? So "Mattaniah the son of Micha, the son of Zabdi, the son of Asaph, the leader . . . began the thanksgiving with prayer" (Neh. 11:17).

There are times when we are to call the people of God together and celebrate with prayers and songs of thanksgiving for all that He has done in our communities. The book of Psalms is full of examples of times of such celebratory gatherings to thank the Lord God Almighty for His faithfulness, deliverance, salvation and help.

Not only is this appropriate in those special moments of God's help, but it also is always the privilege of leaders who stand in the forefront of the spiritual battles in which our cities are engaged. We must remember that the task of rebuilding our cities is not impossible with God's help through prayer. Should we not, then, be mindful to enter into His gates with thanksgiving in our hearts?

Note

1. Jacques Ellul, *Meaning of the City* (Grand Rapids, Mich.: Eerdmans, 1970), p. 16.

Chapter Twelve

ENFORCING THE PRINCIPLES
OF SPIRITUAL WARFARE

Dr. Charles Doolittle *is a police officer with the Glendale, California, police department and associate pastor for prayer at Jubilee Church of Camarillo, California.*

In Matthew 12:25-29, Jesus addresses the religious minds of His day on an issue that is essential to the destruction, dispersing and displacing of opposition to the kingdom of God. His first statement is critical: "Every kingdom divided against itself is brought to desolation." The key word is "divided." If division is successful, a kingdom will fall.

Is it possible that we who are members of the kingdom of God could help bring about division and hence the downfall of the kingdom of Satan? If so, how would we go about it?

Jesus said that if you are going to enter someone else's property or kingdom, you must first "bind the strong man" (v. 29). This is both a natural and a spiritual law. I know it works in law enforcement. Robbers do this especially in home invasion robberies or bank robberies. The thieves will tie up either the head of the household (mother or father) or whoever poses the greatest threat of opposition to the robbers' task.

This does exactly what it is designed to do: It brings fear to those with the strongman. Once the thieves have accomplished the goal of binding the strongman, or head of the place, they are able to spoil his house, or "kingdom," to take what is under his dominion.

The Importance of Authority

Two critical things must take place in order to complete a binding or loosing. First, a person must be in close proximity to the individual he or she is going to bind or loose (as in the case of handcuffs). And second, the one who does the binding must be in a position of authority.

A fascinating illustration of the importance of authority in binding the strongman Satan is recorded in Acts 19:13-16:

Then some of the itinerant Jewish exorcists took it upon themselves to call the name of the Lord Jesus over those who had evil spirits, saying, "We exorcise you by the Jesus whom Paul preaches." Also there were seven sons of Sceva, a Jewish chief priest, who did so. And the evil spirit answered and said, "Jesus I know, and Paul I know; but who are you?" Then the man in whom the evil spirit was leaped on them, overpowered them, and prevailed

against them, so that they fled out of that house naked
and wounded.

Why did the demonic powers turn on these would-be exorcists?
Because the exorcists had no position of authority. They were
not ambassadors from heaven, nor were they the Son of the
Most High.

Now, in the natural world, where do the police get the
authority to arrest? For me, it is from laws found in the
California Penal Code and, ultimately, in the U.S. Constitution.
Without the established laws of the United States, peace officers
could never arrest (bind) any person.

By the same token, the children of God will never bind the
devil without the authority of the Lord Jesus. Without His victory on Calvary and over hell, we could not bind the devil or his
activities. Why? Because we would not have the authority He
conferred on us when He conquered Satan and commissioned
us to bind the enemy in His name (see Mark 16:17).

I have had many ministry opportunities over the last three
years to serve on ministry and prayer teams with competent and
proficient deliverance and intercessory prayer leaders. There
were times when we literally had to go toe to toe with demonic
powers. The power to bring deliverance occurs as we minister in
Jesus' name and access the authority required to bring freedom.

As a licensed police officer, I have seen others who are reluctant to make an arrest. Some are afraid of getting into an alter-
cation with a suspect. These persons are obviously in the wrong
business!

The same principle applies to the believer and intercessor.
You cannot be afraid or intimidated by Satan's threats. You
must stand up to him and not allow him to prosper. At some
point you must bind the strongman.

Jesus promised that whatever His followers bind on earth will be bound in heaven (see Matt. 18:18). To bind means to tie. The Greek term here is from the word *deo*, and implies firm restriction or necessity. It is the same as the root word in Luke 13:16, where Jesus says a demonized woman who had had a physical disability for 18 years should be "loosed [untied] from this bond." The woman was literally *tied up with a spirit.* Satan had restricted her freedom; but as a "daughter of Abraham" she was in covenant relationship with God, where Satan had no authority. Since she needed someone with the authority of heaven to untie her, Jesus did so, because her binding was not bound or decreed in heaven.

WE HAVE BEEN AUTHORIZED BY THE LORD HIMSELF TO BIND AND TO LOOSE—TO TIE UP SATAN AND HIS HELPERS AND TO LOOSE HIS VICTIMS.

Similarly, as people commissioned by Christ, we have been authorized by the Lord Himself to bind and to loose—to tie up Satan and his helpers and to loose his victims. Jesus grants us tremendous authorization, responsibility and power. He gives us this right based on what is occurring (or not occurring) in heaven. If sickness is not in heaven or is not permitted by God, then we have been authorized to bind it up and release God's people from sickness.

Praying As Free Persons in Christ

Physical and mental disabilities are not the only indication that the enemy binds God's people. Even more people are bound by the chains of sin. Others are literally bound or restricted, such as those who are incarcerated. Still others, such as black Americans' ancestors, were in bondage as slaves for hundreds of years.

Unfortunately, some still seem to be shackled to this past. Even though they have been long since emancipated, they have never recovered to walk in freedom. They have not fully realized the truth that Jesus came to "preach deliverance to the captives" (Luke 4:18, *KJV*). They have not affirmed for themselves that since Christ has come, we are now set free. Yet Jesus states this again and again: "You shall know the truth, and the truth shall make you free" (John 8:32). And, "If the Son makes you free, you shall be free indeed" (v. 36).

The interesting thing about the black community is that we have the ability to overcome major adversity, setbacks and injustice; but too often we show by our attitudes and actions that we still have a slave, or bondage, mentality. What I believe God wants from us as we advance to the next stage of liberty is to overcome this mentality.

How do we do this? It involves the process of walking out and living the victory of Calvary, and abiding in the Vine. The Bible states plainly that Jesus won for us the victory when He died on the cross. And Jesus states very plainly that He is "the vine," adding that "If you abide in Me, and My words abide in you, you will ask what you desire, and it shall be done for you" (John 15:5,7).

The many slaves who were brought to this country certainly "asked," using the avenue of prayer to overcome ill treatment, bondage and a hostile nation to rise to the place where we are today. Abiding in Christ throughout the fiery trials that have beset black Christians has equipped us to use the weapon of prayer effectively—as free men and women in Christ. It is the effectual fervent prayer of the righteous that avails much (see Jas. 5:16).

Freedom Is a Decision

I think we forget one of the reasons Jesus came to this planet. He brought the ways of the Father to show us a higher way of living—how to live in freedom by defeating the devil and ruling in Christ's strength over circumstances of this life. All this is implied in His statement in Matthew 18:18 that "whatever you bind on earth will be bound in heaven, and whatever you loose on earth will be loosed in heaven."

The *Amplified Bible* replaces "bind" with "whatever you forbid and declare to be improper and unlawful." There must be a *declaration* in order to bind something. Since Jesus declared our freedom, we, too, are to make the decision to declare it and to live in it. We are literally to declare that living as bound instead of free is unlawful in the heavens.

I believe this is why Jesus "went about doing good and healing all who were oppressed by the devil" (Acts 10:38). He was declaring that evil and unauthorized sickness were "unlawful" in heaven, and in turn giving us the authority to do good and to loose Satan's binding authority on earth as well. The things Jesus did on the earth, we are authorized by the Father in heaven to continue.

In this, Jesus gives tremendous authority to the individual and the Church. Of course it should be understood that we can do nothing without abiding in Christ. Whatever we declare lawful must already be declared lawful in heaven. But heaven *has* declared that we are free, so we are not to allow the devil to stop anyone from acting on that declaration.

For example, when I was working as an investigator dealing primarily with gang members, in one particular case a mother wanted me to talk to her daughter and redirect her from the gang member she was dating. There were times during their dating relationship when the gang member would beat this young lady and keep her confined against her will. This abusive and destructive relationship went on for nearly two years.

Finally, this young girl said, "Enough is enough. I want to go home!" She called her mother and said, "Mom, I'm ready to come home." And she did. This young lady went back to school, got good grades and has since graduated. She is absolutely beautiful—and she is free. You see, the devil cannot hold anyone in his grasp if the person wants to be free.

Measuring Satan's Size

Another thing I have learned both in law enforcement and from being involved in spiritual warfare is that when you set out to bind the strongman it is wise to bring along enough help to succeed, depending on his size and the size of his empire. As Jesus said, we cannot expect to enter a strongman's house and spoil his goods unless we first bind him (see Matt. 12:29). The bigger the strongman, the more help you will need to bind him and declare the victory.

When law enforcement officers put into effect a search warrant at a high-risk location (meaning that there is a chance for evidence to be lost or the suspect to flee), they take certain measures. First, they use the element of surprise to assault the location. Second, when they enter the place to be searched, everyone present is detained. Each person gets bound until the police are reasonably sure they have the strongman/bad guy bound. Then they look for the goods, or the "spoil."

It should be a source of tremendous courage to us as Christians that we have the presence of Christ helping us with these measures to effect the arrest!

But did you know that law enforcement persons do not ever *have* to effect an arrest if they do not want to? I did not say it would be in their best interest not to make an arrest, but technically they are not required to do so. Even though they are trained and given the proper equipment, they still do not have to effect an arrest.

Likewise, many of us in the Body of Christ never get beyond the training-officer syndrome in "effecting the arrest" of the strongmen in our lives. Sometimes we choose to allow fear or the bondage of traumatic occurrences from the past to cause us to stay in a bound condition or state of mind.

Take courage from the fact that because Christ has set you free and established freedom as heaven's domain, you can bind the strongman in your life, declaring his actions unlawful.

The opposite end of this statement is that if we do *not* bind the strongman, he will continue to act unlawfully and destructively. The Father has sent His Son, who spoiled the principalities and powers and recaptured the territory they occupied. Jesus has defeated the devil and death. Now we must enforce the victory of Calvary.

The Power of Teamwork

Although I have emphasized the authority of the individual Christian in asserting his or her power in Christ over the strongmen, this does not mean we do not need others to stand with us in larger operations.

One of the keys I believe is necessary in binding and spoiling the kingdom of the strongman Satan is the unity of the Body of Christ. Some of the weapons the strongman uses to render us ineffective against his kingdom are disunity, discord, disobedience and pride. As a race—what the Greek New Testament calls an ethnos—African-Americans must operate strategically to divide and displace the kingdom of darkness by operating also as an agent of unity in the kingdom of God on earth.

We have many people in the Body of Christ who are addressing principalities and sometimes even ruling spirits over nations, either on their own or as individual churches. We must be extremely cautious with this approach. The extent of such principalities and powers usually calls for help.

You can see this even in the natural realm. Many nations of the world have been called on to restrain the power of the strongman in the nation of Iraq. The leader of the Iraqi military and nation, as small as it is, needs to be opposed, not just by one nation, but by multiple nations committed to bringing his activities under control.

Likewise, the Body of Christ, not just the individual Christian, is empowered by the Holy Spirit and has the authority of Jesus and the "power of attorney" to use His name to overthrow anything in Satan's arsenal. But to try and launch an assault on territorial demonic powers without appropriate consultation with the larger Body, as well as adequate consecration and training, is very foolish.

OUR GREATEST TRIUMPH WILL COME AS WE UNITE RACIALLY, DENOMINATIONALLY AND THEOLOGICALLY AROUND THE NAME OF THE LORD JESUS.

It is my opinion and observation that our greatest triumph will come as we unite racially, denominationally and theologically around the name of the Lord Jesus. It is here where I believe we will see a tremendous release of God's power and a disruption and fall of the demonic powers over a city, county, state and nation.

Words of Caution

In connection with "territorial spirits," many people fail to recognize in this dispensation of revelation regarding spiritual warfare that Jesus dealt very little with demonic powers over regions and territories. Instead, He focused on demons who were housed in the bodies of persons.

In Mark 5 is the story of the demonized person of Gadara. When the demons in him realized that their activity was threatened by the presence of Jesus, they asked to be allowed to enter a herd of pigs feeding near the mountains. Jesus did not deal with the ruling spirit of the region but with the local spirits in the swine. Why?

One reason was the tendency for demons who were cast out of persons to take up residence in them again if they were not infused with more positive influences (see Matt. 12:43-45). Because the gospel had not been fully preached in the region of Gadara, it would have been in a worse condition than before if Jesus had just removed a demon with regionwide power without adequate teaching to fill the void.

In order for us to be successful in taking our cities and surrounding territories from the strongman, the gospel must be preached throughout the territory, and Christ's ruling authority must be established in the region. It is similar to the principle of the Israelites overthrowing and driving out the occupants of the Promised Land little by little. It is sometimes wiser to take small steps toward victory.

Regional Spirits

We do see some activity among Christ's followers in dealing with regional spirits. In Acts 16, Paul and Silas dealt with what at first appears to be just another demonized woman. But what we really see is the removal of a territorial spirit.

> Now it happened, as we went to prayer, that a certain slave girl possessed with a spirit of divination met us, who brought her masters much profit by fortune-telling. This girl followed Paul and us, and cried out, saying, "These men are the servants of the Most High God, who proclaim to us the way of salvation." And this she did for many days. But Paul, greatly annoyed, turned and said to the spirit, "I command you in the name of Jesus Christ to come out of her." And he came out that very hour (Acts 16:16-18).

When those who used the woman's demonic powers for profit saw that the source of their income had dried up, they caused a riot and Paul and Silas wound up in jail. We can therefore recognize the spirit occupying the body of this woman as the ruling spirit of the region because it controlled the monetary system and the "religious" people.

When you see these kinds of angry responses to acts of goodness within your city, you have probably found and touched the ruling territorial spirit. This is an issue that many people forget when they become involved in spiritual warfare. The devil does not just sit by and allow us, without retaliation, to "spoil his house"—that is, to redeem from his clutches those who are under his dominion.

Breaking Free from the Spirit of Poverty

Among the people of God in general and people of color in particular, many are bound with a poverty mentality. This binding severely limits us in what we can do, where we can go and when we go where we need to go. We must break the bondage of poverty to assist in the promotion and financing of the gospel in this nation and around the world.

The devil continues to try to ensure that we never rise above the level of poverty or at least that we never rise above being able to meet bare necessities, either in fact or in our minds. He wants to keep us in the bondage of feeling that we are poverty-stricken.

Returning to the woman who had been "bent over" for 18 years, Jesus asked His critics, "Ought not this woman, being a daughter of Abraham, whom Satan has bound . . . be loosed from this bond?" (Luke 13:16). Now, according to the law of double reference principle of interpretation, we could say that the woman was bound spiritually. But the Abrahamic Covenant she was under was more than a spiritual one. Being related to Abraham spiritually meant that earthly physical needs were also included as a part of the Covenant provision. I submit to you that Satan bound or limited her in both the spiritual and the physical realms.

Therefore, when the woman was loosed from her bondage— made free by the One in authority—she was not only liberated from satanic influence but also able to do more physically and to help herself financially. Her vision about herself changed. "Therefore if the Son makes you free, you shall be free indeed" (John 8:36).

According to Galatians 3, we are also the seed of Abraham and heirs according to the promise (v. 29). As children of the Covenant, it is as much our job to act on our release from bondage as it is to bind the devil. We spend entirely too much time focusing on what Satan did, what he is doing or what he has done. We should be focused on the Creator and what He did, is doing and will do—including His intent to provide us with whatever material blessings we need to further the work of His kingdom.

Praying with Power

Let us return to a second passage in Matthew where Jesus promised us the power to bind and loose on earth whatever has been authorized by heaven. As we saw earlier in Matthew 18, the individual believer is given authority in Jesus' name. In the other passage, Matthew 16, Jesus adds a special word to Peter:

> And I also say to you that you are Peter, and on this rock I will build My church, and the gates of Hades shall not prevail against it. And I will give you the keys of the kingdom of heaven, and whatever you bind on earth will be bound in heaven, and whatever you loose on earth will be loosed in heaven (Matt. 16:18,19).

Here Jesus adds a word of promise to be imprinted in our hearts: No matter how hard Satan and "the gates of Hades" try in their efforts to destroy Kingdom people, our power to bind them will prevail.

Let's note how this is illustrated in Acts 12:5-7. King Herod had bound the apostle Peter and put him in jail. (The word for "bound" used here is the same word used in Jesus' promise to give us the power to bind the strongman.) Meanwhile, unceasing prayer or intercession is made for Peter (v. 5). It is this kind of praying that unlocks and releases God's power (Greek *dynamis*— miracle-working, divine power). In this case it also releases a member of the angelic host, who overpowered the guards and the chains and the entire prison to escort Peter to freedom!

This powerful account is an illustration of the failure of the gates of hell to prevail against or to overpower the Church. The fact is that Herod had bound the wrong people—people living in the power of the kingdom of God—in his attempt to spread his evil control.

Although Satan failed in this attempt, he still tries to enter into the Church through fear, intimidation and eventually death. But understand this: Jesus said that whatever we bind will be bound, and whatever we loose will be loosed; and the gates of hell (Hades) will not overpower the Kingdom. The issue is whether or not, in the face of such powerful promises, we are going to become fearful and intimidated by the attacks of an impotent strong man.

This tremendous revelation is similar to the power delegated to those who are in law enforcement. Once we have been authorized (as police officers, sheriffs and the like), we then have the backing (the power) of the state and of the U.S. Constitution to assist us in enforcing the law.

Without this power, lawlessness would reign in the land. And without the authority (*exousia*) and power (*dynamis*) of God behind Christians, the kingdom of heaven would be doomed; and we would be unable to overcome the kingdom of darkness. With it, however, the gates of hell will not prevail against the Church!

"Let Him Go!"

Another illustration of this principle is in John 11—the story of Jesus' raising His friend Lazarus from the dead. We recall that Lazarus's sisters sent for Jesus after their brother became sick and that he died before Jesus arrived. By the time Jesus came,

Lazarus had been dead for a few days and the decaying process had begun. But Jesus called him out of the tomb anyway. And when Lazarus emerged, still bound by the grave wrappings, Jesus made this staggering statement to those present: "Loose him, and let him go" (v. 44).

With the natural mind we casually read this and think, of course we would loose him. But I believe the Holy Spirit wants us to see a deeper principle here. Jesus said that whatever *we* loose on earth will be loosed in heaven. And notice who were the ones to do the loosing at Lazarus's tomb. It was *the people*, not Jesus.

The principle that I believe the Holy Spirit wants us to see is that God has given us the tools and equipment to bring deliverance to the captives. It is up to the Church to get in close proximity and loose people from those things that bind them.

For Lazarus, it was his graveclothes. For the woman in Luke 13, it was a spirit of infirmity. For many in our day it is the spirit of slavery or poverty or sin. I believe the Father wants us to know that we have been given authorization to bind and loose people from all such "graveclothes."

Overcoming the Proximity Problem

Toward the beginning of this chapter it was pointed out that in order to effect an arrest, police officers have to risk close proximity to the suspect. Even in the spiritual realm we are sometimes called to be physically close to those who need to be loosed from the bondage of the strongman. At other times, we need to remember that we can be close in the spirit to those in such needs. Paul said in Ephesians 6:12 that "we do not wrestle against flesh and blood, but against principalities, against powers, against the rulers of the darkness of this age, against spiritual hosts of wickedness in the heavenly places."

Although wrestling is a close-contact sport, we can wrestle spiritually at any distance. There is no time or distance in the realm of the spirit. Stepping out of this life and into eternity is instantaneous. To be absent from the body is to be present with the Lord (see 2 Cor. 5:6).

The Roman centurion who came to Jesus made the great faith statement to Him, "Only speak a word, and my servant will be healed" (Matt. 8:8). Despite Jesus' being absent from the servant's bedside, the Bible says that the healing was accomplished according to the centurion's faith. Jesus merely spoke the word and it was done.

Divine Resources

Prayer also unleashes the hosts of heaven against powers we cannot confront in the flesh. We worship a God who has "ministering spirits sent forth to minister for those who will inherit salvation" (Heb. 1:14). We who proclaim and declare the Word of the Lord can actually release angels to work on our behalf!

On the night of Jesus' betrayal, the soldiers arrested Jesus. As they were taking Him away, Peter cut off the ear of the high priest's servant (see John 18:10). Jesus healed the man's ear but then declared that He could have called 12 legions of angels if He had wanted (see Matt. 26:53). Who would have done the fighting? The angelic host!

To overthrow resistance, whether in combat or on our streets, the military or the police often call for reinforcements. If my agency does not have the resources, we will call an adjacent city. If they aren't enough, we will call another. And if more are still needed, we will call the next agency and so on until the problem is under our control and dominion.

As Christians, we too can call for divine reinforcements if we need them to secure a place or position in a territory and overthrow the resistance. If the churches in one area are not large enough or numerous enough to proclaim victory, then those churches should notify the World Prayer Center in Colorado (719-536-9100), who will notify intercessors around the planet in a matter of minutes. These hosts will pray until breakthrough comes and we have the situation in hand.

Such resources assure our success, whether immediately or in the future, as we who are engaged in spiritual warfare march forward, binding and loosing and advancing the kingdom of God.

More on Prayer & Spiritual Warfare

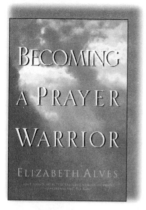

A Guide to Effective
and Powerful Prayer
Elizabeth Alves
Paperback
ISBN 08307.23331

Foreword by Tim and
Beverly LaHaye
Quin Sherrer with Ruthanne Garlock
Paperback
ISBN 08307.22017

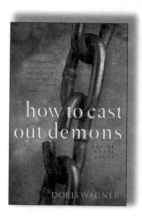

A Guide to the Basics
Doris Wagner
Paperback
ISBN 08307.25350

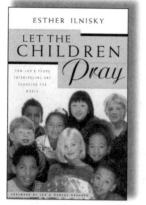

How God's Young Intercessors
Are Changing the World
Esther Ilnisky
Paperback
ISBN 08307.25245

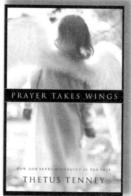

How God Sends His Angels
as You Pray
Thetus Tenney
Paperback
ISBN 08307.24656

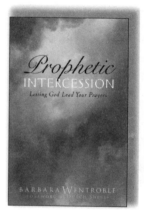

Letting God Lead Your Prayers
Barbara Wentroble
Paperback
ISBN 08307.23765

More on Prayer & Spiritual Warfare

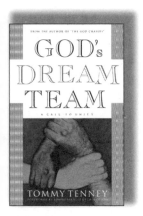

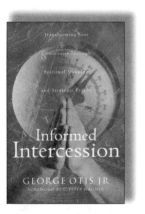

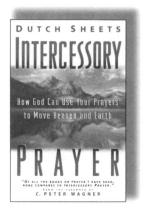

A Call to Unity
Tommy Tenney
Paperback
ISBN 08307.23846

Transforming Your Community
Through Spiritual Mapping and
Strategic Prayer
George Otis, Jr.
Paperback
ISBN 08307.19377

How God Can Use Your Prayers
to Move Heaven and Earth
Dutch Sheets
Paperback
ISBN 08307.19008

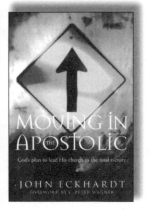

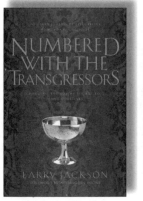

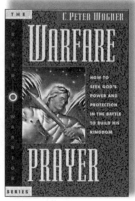

God's Plan to Lead His Church
to the Final Victory
John Eckhardt
Paperback
ISBN 08307.23730

Changing the Way We See the
Lost–and Ourselves
Larry Jackson
Paperback
ISBN 08307.21967

How to Seek God's Power
and Protection in the Battle
to Build His Kingdom
C. Peter Wagner
Paperback
ISBN 08307.15134

Available at your local Christian bookstore.
www.regalbooks.com

041800